The Political Structur
1949-1999

Media, Democracy & Political Process Series

Edited by Christian Herzog, Volker Grassmuck,
Christian Heise and Orkan Torun

The Political Structure of UK Broadcasting 1949–1999

David Elstein

meson press

**Bibliographical Information of the
German National Library**
The German National Library lists this publication in the
Deutsche Nationalbibliografie (German National Biblio-
graphy); detailed bibliographic information is available
online at http://dnb.d-nb.de

Published in 2015 by meson press, Hybrid Publishing Lab,
Centre for Digital Cultures, Leuphana University of Lüneburg
www.meson-press.com

Design concept: Torsten Köchlin, Silke Krieg
Cover Image: Sebastian Mühleis and Christian Herzog
The print edition of this book is printed by Lightning Source,
Milton Keynes, United Kingdom

ISBN (Print):   978-3-95796-060-3
ISBN (PDF):   978-3-95796-061-0
ISBN (EPUB): 978-3-95796-062-7
DOI: 10.14619/011

The digital editions of this publication can be downloaded
freely at: www.meson-press.com

Funded by the EU major project Innovation Incubator
Lüneburg

This Publication is licensed under the CC-BY-SA 4.0 International. To view a copy of this license, visit:
http://creativecommons.org/licenses/by-sa/4.0/

Contents

Foreword by the Series Editors 9
Foreword by the Author 17

[1]   **Beveridge 23**

[2]   **Pilkington 45**

[3]   **Annan 65**

[4]   **Hunt 85**

[5]   **Peacock 107**

[6]   **After Peacock: The Politics Of Digital 131**

[7]   **Davies and the Digital Licence Fee 159**

[8]   **The BBC in the Digital Century 183**

Foreword by the Series Editors

The inspiration for publishing this book has its origins in the early stages of my PhD research, a comparative study of British and German media and communication policies, at Loughborough University. The research relied on a mixture of elite interviews and archival records. With regard to the former, my approach was to outline key processes and events in British and German media and communications policy and to then identify the key figures instrumental in shaping the respective developments at crucial historical junctures and points in time.[1] In 2007, when designing a first list of possible informants, my PhD supervisor Peter Golding suggested I contact David Elstein, who responded swiftly and sent me his Oxford Lectures. I found the lecture series extremely useful and still regard it as an authoritative source on the history of British broadcasting policy. The lectures were never published and I am grateful for having a chance to make them available to a wider readership.

In his seminal work *Media and Power* James Curran (2000) presents British media history as a series of competing narratives.[2] David Elstein's narrative champions individual choice and economic freedom. With regard to the funding of the BBC Elstein is a strong advocate of subscription, a policy measure advocated by some authors affiliated with the Institute of Economic Affairs (IEA) since the 1960s (e.g. Caine 1966,1968; Veljanovski and Bishop 1983).[3] David Elstein has made a case for a coherent alternative rationale for funding public service content through a contestable fund (see e.g. Elstein 1991, 2000, 2005).[4] Normative assumptions that public service broadcasters create market distortions and inefficiencies in the amount of public money spent in creating public value underpin his rigorous, at times revisionist, analysis.

This publication has been made possible by the EU Innovation Incubator at Leuphana University Lüneburg, a major research-driven project for regional development with a total volume of EUR 98 million running from 2010 to 2015, funded by the European Regional Development Fund (ERDF) and the State of Lower Saxony. The Innovation Incubator is a unique project designed to create enduring economic effects in the areas of sustainable energy, health, and digital media. Roughly, the Incubator area of digital media can be subdivided into three projects concerned with public service broadcasting (Public Service Media 2.0 Lab), publishing (Hybrid Publishing Lab) and gamification (Gamification Lab). These projects develop under the umbrella of the Centre for Digital Cultures (CDC), which will persist beyond the funding period.[5] The flagship project of the Hybrid Publishing Lab is meson press, and I would like to thank my meson press colleagues Sebastian Mühleis, Marcus Burkhardt and Andreas Kirchner for the many hours they invested in this project.

The series *Media, Democracy & Political Process* was launched by members of the Public Service Media 2.0 Lab, namely Volker Grassmuck, Christian Heise (Hybrid Publishing Lab), Orkan Torun and myself. It sets out to address the impacts of digitisation on politics, culture and society and explores how the emergence of digital communication affects established modes of policy-making and representation as well as socio-cultural values, identities and networks. Amongst the questions that publications appearing in the series seek to answer are: What consequences arise from the digital shift for traditional political institutions and processes of decision-making and for the media and communication systems in twenty-first century democracies? What new opportunities and risks are posed by digital technologies in terms of civic engagement and more transparent and inclusive policy-making processes? Which new forms of public sphere, social change and cultural techniques are evolving? These and related questions are addressed from a variety of perspectives, incorporating historical approaches and cross-country comparative research.

The series seeks to publish original research and contributions by experts and practitioners from the fields of politics, civil society, non-governmental organisations and regulatory agencies. It aims to contribute to the lively discourse on political and social implications of digital media technologies while working towards models and options for addressing current socio-political and -cultural challenges.

Christian Herzog

Endnotes

1. Potschka, Christian. *Towards a Market in Broadcasting: Communications Policy in the UK and Germany*. Basingstoke: Palgrave Macmillan, 2012, 8.
2. Curran, James. *Media and Power*. London: Routledge, 2002.
3. Caine, Sir Sydney. *Prices for Primary Producers*. London: Institute of Economic Affairs, 1966; Caine, Sir Sydney. *Paying for TV?*. London: Institute for Economic Affairs, 1968; Veljanovski, Cento G. and Bishop, William D. *Choice by Cable: The Economics of a New Era in Television*. London: Institute for Economic Affairs, 1983.
4. Elstein, David. "Competing with the Public Sector in Broadcasting." *Economic Affairs* 20, no. 4 (2000): 13–20; Elstein, David. "The James MacTaggart Lecture 1991. The Future of Television: Market Forces and Social Values." In *Television Policy: The MacTaggart Lectures*, edited by Bob Franklin, 147–155. Edinburgh: Edinburgh University Press, 2005; Elstein, David. "Public Service Broadcasting in the Digital Age." *Economic Affairs* 25, no. 4 (2005): 68–70.
5. Beyes, Timon, Christian Herzog and Christian Heise. Forthcoming. "Centre for Digital Cultures." In *The Sage International Encyclopedia of Mass Media & Society*, edited by Debra Merskin. Thousand Oaks, CA: Sage.

Foreword by the Author

Being invited to publish lectures delivered many years previously is a double-edged sword. At one level, it is pleasing for material which found only a small audience at the time to be made generally available. At another level, the risk of finding one's old judgements to have been overtaken by events or subsequent scholarship is a little unnerving.

Fortunately, few people in academia have chosen to compare and contrast the unusual British phenomenon of regularly examining the broadcasting options faced by society, with major reports (if we exclude the more limited inquiry by Lord Hunt) every ten to fifteen years after 1945 (Beveridge in 1950, Pilkington in 1962, Annan in 1977 and Peacock in 1986). At the time the lectures were delivered, in 1999, it was not clear whether a review of the BBC's finances that year, led by economist Gavyn Davies, would be a full survey – expanding, as Peacock had, well beyond its limited brief – or more like Hunt in its narrow focus. If Davies kept to his brief, I fully expected a new major review to be commissioned.

It never happened. Thirty years on, despite massive changes in the technology and ecology of broadcasting, no UK government has felt the need – as one politician dismissively described the process – to pull up the plant in order to examine its roots. Instead, the regulator created in the 2003 Communications Act, Ofcom, has from time to time reported on public service broadcasting (PSB), even as the sector it directly regulates – the commercial public service channels, ITV, Channel 4 and Five – steadily ran down its PSB supply. Frustratingly, Ofcom has no leverage over the BBC, which is responsible for 90% of all PSB output. Meanwhile, successive reviews of the BBC's Charter have largely ignored the wider PSB context that the four major reports from the post-war years had addressed.

In 2003, at the invitation of the then Shadow Secretary of State for Culture, Media and Sport, John Whittingdale, I set up the

Broadcasting Policy Group, which published a report on the future of the BBC, "Beyond The Charter," explicitly placing its recommendations in the context of the growing crisis in PSB.[1] In a surprise appointment after the May 2015 election, Whittingdale was given the actual job of Secretary of State. He had, just in February, led a House of Commons Select Committee inquiry into the future of the BBC. It will be interesting to see what parts of that Committee's report, or indeed the BPG's report, find their way into government policy as the BBC seeks to negotiate a new Charter for 2017.

My Oxford Lectures lack the kind of formal apparatus (references, footnotes, sources) that academics these days would expect. They were written to be delivered and heard, with only the underlying reports being assumed to be required reading. If my citing of contemporary newspaper and parliamentary responses to the reports, without specific references, causes frustration, I can only apologise. My own academic training – at Cambridge in the early 1960s – required me to write essays that I read out loud to my supervisor. In post-academic life, I have given dozens of public lectures, many of them "named" (Goodman, Raymond Williams, Reed, Swinton, Bernard Simons), including inaugurals as a visiting professor at universities, and never attached a single footnote. I invite readers of these Oxford Lectures to imagine they are in an English Faculty lecture room: no slides, no reading notes, just a lectern and a text.

After delivering the six English Faculty lectures in February and March of 1999, I was invited back to Oxford by another cross-disciplinary group to deliver two more: one on the report from the committee chaired by Gavyn Davies, published that summer, and another on the BBC in the digital age. By contrast with the first six, these lectures are much more engaged with the broadcasting politics of the moment: although I link back to the themes of the earlier lectures, the detailed political twists and turns predominate. For that, I make no apology.

When I left Cambridge, I was offered the equivalent of a general traineeship at the BBC (although I had acquired a double first in History, I was too young, at 19, to be offered an actual traineeship, for which the minimum age was 21). I was seconded for a year to the Centre for Contemporary Cultural Studies, at Birmingham University, under the supervision of Richard Hoggart and Stuart Hall, where I wrote a short thesis on the concept of public service broadcasting. It was an opportunity to read widely and deeply, soon after the publication of the Pilkington Report, which Hoggart had so substantially influenced, into the wide variety of ideas inside and outside the BBC about the purposes of broadcasting.

Looking back, not just 16 years to when the Oxford Lectures were delivered, but 50 years before that to the time of Beveridge, it is impossible not to marvel at the vast changes that have overtaken broadcasting since the 1940s, and the earnest debate then over whether the BBC's broadcasting monopoly should be maintained. Perhaps a "philosophy" of broadcasting is simply not an option in so complex an environment: but how the "great and the good" addressed the issues of broadcasting in the 1950s, 1960s, 1970s and 1980s, and how their main recommendations failed to be implemented, time after time, remains a fascinating phenomenon, even as those recommendations fade into history.

David Elstein
July 2015

Endnotes
1. Broadcasting Policy Group. *Beyond the Charter: The BBC after 2006*. London: Premium Publishing, 2004. https://archive.org/details/BeyondTheCharter.

Introduction

Fifty years ago, the first of the post-war committees of inquiry into broadcasting was created. Chaired by Lord Beveridge, it addressed the central issue of whether to sustain the BBC's monopoly of radio and television services. All but one of its members rejected the various suggestions for ending the monopoly. The Labour government broadly agreed. Yet such was the procrastination displayed by ministers – both in creating the Beveridge Committee and then in responding to its recommendations – that before the BBC's Charter (and monopoly) could be quietly renewed, the 1951 election dislodged Labour.

Most of the incoming Conservative cabinet were equally well disposed to the BBC's monopoly, but the Beveridge Committee's minority report in favour of breaking the monopoly had been written by a Conservative backbencher, J Selwyn Lloyd, who now found his arguments strongly supported by a hardworking group of sympathizers within the new House of Commons. The cabinet's "fixer", Lord Woolton, found a seemingly neat solution to the split within his own party: radio (the important medium) would remain a BBC monopoly, but the sideshow of television would not.

So the pattern was set – of finding a political structure for broadcasting through the medium of committees of inquiry, and then for key recommendations of the committee reports to be overtaken by the law of unintended consequences.

After 1949, three further committees of inquiry into broadcasting were appointed, each taking up to two years to complete its work: Pilkington, which reported in 1962; Annan, which reported in 1977; and Peacock, which reported in 1986. In addition, a 3-man committee of inquiry chaired by Lord Hunt conducted a rapid six-month survey in 1982 on the impact of cable television on broadcasting policy.

If Beveridge, unintentionally, led to the creation of a second television channel, Pilkington and Annan were explicitly invited to adjudicate on the allocation of additional channels, as more spectrum was made available for broadcast purposes. Yet the main thrust of both reports failed to strike home.

Pilkington found the ITV service – established in 1955 – so deficient that it recommended reducing the franchise holders to mere programme suppliers, with the key functions of commissioning, scheduling and airtime-selling undertaken by the ITV regulator, the ITA. This might have appealed to the Labour Party, at that point still nominally committed to the abolition of ITV. However, the Conservative government of the day – even if it could stomach Pilkington's allocation of the third channel to the BBC – inevitably resisted a high-minded, socialistic restructuring of the whole of ITV so soon after its launch.

Annan's reversal was more directly a result of political changes. Lord Annan had been appointed by Labour before the 1970 election, was stood down after the Conservatives unexpectedly returned to power, and was then re-appointed when Labour recaptured office. The Annan Report decisively rejected ITV's bid for the fourth available television channel, as a balance against the BBC's two-pronged service. Instead, Annan proposed an Open Broadcasting Authority, pursuing an essentially educational mission. However, yet again, Labour indecision left a policy vacuum, which the Conservatives promptly filled once they won the 1979 election.

The OBA was abandoned. Yet, by a quirk of history, the two new Home Office ministers, William Whitelaw and Leon Brittan, also abandoned the Conservative manifesto commitment to an ITV2. Instead, a high water mark in political and social engineering was achieved in the creation of a quasi-commercial alternative Channel Four, with a structure uncannily similar to that recommended by Pilkington in 1962 for ITV.

This was the last fling of cultural policy-making in the field of broadcasting. The notion that broadcast spectrum was scarce and had to be allocated according to social needs, not market logic, had prevailed long after the age of rationing had ended elsewhere in the UK, and with it the assumption that the man in Whitehall knows best. Now, technology was to erode the scarcity argument, and the two committees of inquiry of the 1980s adopted a new approach, consumer-driven rather than provider-driven.

The Hunt Report of 1982 attempted to counter Annan's largely negative view of cable as a potential medium for pay-television. For Annan – as for the broadcast establishment – cable would be socially divisive if it diverted programming and revenue away from free-to-air television. Hunt urged a liberal regulatory regime for cable, and Tory ministers – especially those with a technology brief – eagerly embraced its findings. However, yet again policy was unexpectedly thrown off course – changes in the Treasury treatment of capital allowances stifled cable's development. Ironically, it was only re-kindled by the failure of yet another government-sponsored, technologically-driven initiative: high-powered satellite television, which was dislodged by a medium-powered satellite alternative that finally delivered the programming stream so desperately needed for cable's growth.

Peacock was perhaps the most dramatic example of a committee that both broke its political framework and then saw key recommendations ignored. Set up to report on the financing of the BBC, and packed with free-market economists, Peacock defeated all expectations by rejecting advertising and sponsorship as alternatives to the licence fee, and instead advocating the long term replacement of the fee by subscription.

Blithely ignoring its remit, Peacock then addressed commercial television, recommending wholesale reform: auctioning of ITV licences; separation of Channel Four's airtime selling from ITV's; and substantial access to ITV's schedules for independent producers. Initially consigned to the long political grass as impractical, Peacock prevailed with the cabinet radicals, and these key recommendations were all implemented.

20 Yet the pattern of the past prevailed in other ways. The Peacock Report's first recommendation was for a simple device to be installed in all new television sets so as to ease the eventual introduction of encrypted television services. This was never implemented – much to the cost of today's consumers – thanks to a consultant's report for the Home Office that demonstrated (embarrassingly wrongly, as it turned out) why subscription funding of television would not work. Another key recommendation – for freedom of speech within the law – saw Thatcherite economics out-flanked by Thatcherite morality, with the creation instead of yet another regulatory watchdog, the Broadcasting Standards Council.

Perhaps most surprisingly, the far-sighted Peacock Report failed to spot the potential for a fifth terrestrial channel, which emerged a mere year later. Nor, indeed, did the immense potential of medium-powered satellites register. To that extent, Peacock was the most paradoxical of the post-war reports. It dwelt on the distant future, and so missed the near at hand.

More importantly, it placed economic issues above social concerns. It valued freedom more highly than political intervention. It side-stepped the earnest disquisitions on broadcasting philosophy that characterized its predecessors. In effect, it put committees of inquiry into broadcasting out of business. If technological constraints were disappearing, and if consumers could function within an open market, there was less and less room or reason for political structuring of broadcasting.

Since 1986, there have indeed been no further major inquiries. Into the political vacuum has stepped the language of the market. The sixth of these lectures describes the new broadcasting landscape, where ITV is now run by three businessmen with no background in broadcasting, where the BBC is deeply engaged in market issues, where brand management is a core value at Channel Four, and where the most potent financial force in British television did not even exist when Peacock reported.

But it will also deal with the improbable re-emergence of political engagement in the structure of broadcasting, as evidenced by the bi-partisan determination to create a digital terrestrial television platform in the UK, in defence of old-style broadcasting (and regulation), even in an age when unlimited spectrum should have rendered largely redundant any role for the political class.

These six lectures attempt to encompass a period of great change, in both politics and broadcasting. In fifty years, assumptions about society, about political control of broadcasting, and about the relationship between viewers as citizens and as consumers have all been transformed. They will deal with the way in which we are governed as well as the way in which broadcasting functions within a mature democracy. They will trace a path rich in ironies as well as in issues that are as resonant today as fifty years ago.

David Elstein
Visiting Professor in Broadcast Media,
University of Oxford,
Hilary Term 1999.

[1]
Beveridge

23 February 1999

Fifty years ago last month, Herbert Morrison announced the setting up of a Committee of Inquiry into Broadcasting. It was to be chaired by Sir Cyril Radcliffe. But within a few months, Sir Cyril was elevated to the Court of Appeal as Lord Radcliffe. His replacement, Lord Beveridge – famed as the father of the Welfare State – was appointed in June 1949.

The BBC was disappointed – Radcliffe had been deputy chairman of its General Advisory Council. Indeed, three years later, he spoke in a crucial House of Lords debate against the idea of commercial television. Yet Beveridge, too, had served on the BBC's General Advisory Council in the 1930s. Certainly, when the Beveridge Report was finally published in January 1951, the BBC's chairman, Lord Simon of Wythenshawe, noted that "we regarded the Report as a great victory; we assumed that our constitution would be continued, substantially unchanged".

Simon's optimism was understandable: all but one member of the Beveridge Committee had upheld the BBC's monopoly, and a majority firmly opposed commercial broadcasting. The White

Paper in response to Beveridge took the same line. Yet barely four years later, ITV had been launched – what Lord Annan, in a subsequent inquiry into broadcasting, described as "the greatest of all changes in the nation's broadcasting system".

How did this change come about? What does it tell us about the process of using committees of inquiry to manage change in broadcasting? And is it fair, in judging the reversal suffered by Beveridge, to dismiss his Report because "it settled precisely nothing" and its practical results were "negligible", as does the official historian of the BBC, Asa Briggs?

In truth, all the post-war committees of inquiry were frustrated in large matters or small, either by changes in government or lack of support for their recommendations. What this series of lectures addresses is how, in the last 50 years, the structure of British broadcasting has been shaped by the interplay between the overt politics of Westminster and the mediated politics of a succession of independent inquiries, of which the first to report was Beveridge.

With Beveridge, the gap between intention and outcome was the largest, but the influence of the arguments rehearsed in its deliberations persisted long after publication. In particular, the issue of the BBC monopoly was resolved by Beveridge in a manner by no means as clear cut as Lord Simon might have wished. Three members of the committee, including Beveridge himself, were willing to support advertising on the BBC. And one member, the Conservative backbench MP Brigadier Selwyn Lloyd, wrote a dissenting opinion which can be read as a blueprint for much of what subsequently happened to British broadcasting.

At the time, little notice was taken of this minority report. As late as 1952, the BBC's first post-war head of television, in a book assessing the first half century of broadcasting, failed to mention Selwyn Lloyd, and consigned his call for the BBC's monopoly to be broken to a single parenthetical sentence.

But Selwyn Lloyd found an echo amongst the Young Turks in his own parliamentary party, who swelled in number after the 1950 and 1951 elections. When the Labour government collapsed before it could implement Beveridge's majority view, the way was open for the minority report to capture the high ground. ITV may have been the unintended legacy of Beveridge: but it is nonetheless its legacy.

And Beveridge represents more than just a single outcome. It set the tone for nearly forty years of such major inquiries, whose existence, whose regularity of appointment and whose continuity of concerns would take on a larger significance collectively than each would have individually.

For the system of committees of inquiry tells us much about the political structure of British broadcasting. It suggests there is an ideal method of organising broadcasting, which a group of the great and the good will be able to divine. It implies that this is a matter for the providers, not the users, of broadcasting to decide. It places broadcasting within a political framework, but appears to insulate it from direct political control.

As we shall see from examining each of the post-war inquiries in turn, their pre-occupations subtly shift as society changes and as more spectrum becomes available. Indeed, each of the first three reports – Beveridge, Pilkington and Annan – led directly or indirectly to the creation of a new television channel. The last two – Hunt and Peacock – by contrast dealt with the implications of an end to spectrum scarcity. As that prospect becomes reality and as a consumer-driven version of broadcasting progressively displaces the provider-driven one, the role for committees of inquiry seems superfluous – there has been none since 1986. That too is part of the theme of these lectures.

Yet just as spectrum scarcity – real or imagined – lingered long after most other forms of post-war rationing had disappeared, so the ideas associated with it prevailed deep into the second half of the century. Indeed, in my final lecture, I will show there is plenty of life left in them still.

The notion that radio spectrum is a scarce public asset, created by international agreements, and to be utilised for the public good, would have struck a sympathetic echo in the 1920s, when public corporations were already in fashion. John Reith's messianic version of public service found a warm response as soon as he became the first general manager of the British Broadcasting Company, which had been set up in 1922 by a group of radio manufacturers eager to sell wireless sets.

Reith himself sat on the first of the four pre-war committees dealing with broadcasting, chaired by Sir Frederick Sykes in 1923. The Sykes Report urged that broadcasting was such a powerful medium, control of it "ought to remain with the state".

Three years later, the Crawford Report of 1926 recommended that the government should purchase all the shares in the BBC, and re-constitute it under Royal Charter, with the proviso that day-to-day operations should remain free of ministerial direction. So the Company became a Corporation.

The Charter carried an obligation for political impartiality, but that had always been implicit in the Post Office broadcasting licence. As the senior Post Office witness to the Sykes Committee noted, the pre-Charter BBC could be as partisan as it wished, but if so, "I am quite sure that the Licence would never be renewed".

Indeed, the problem lay in the other direction. Reith had already shown himself willing in 1926 to throw the BBC's support behind the government in the General Strike, once a hotly contested High Court judgement had been handed down ruling the strike illegal. His famous syllogism argued that "since the BBC was a national institution and since the government in the crisis were acting for the people...the BBC was for the government in the crisis too".

The new arrangements suited Reith perfectly. The Charter forbade the BBC to accept advertising or sponsorship on its programmes, so a potential source of commercial conflict with the press was avoided. He could now use the BBC's de facto monopoly to pursue the social, cultural and religious purposes of broadcasting. As for deciding which politicians would be granted access to the airwaves, during the 1930s that could be safely left to the party leaders. Churchill was from time to time one of the victims of this process.

From 1937, there was an increase in the subvention to the BBC to cover the costs of the overseas service that Reith had launched five years earlier, so clearly was it seen to be meeting Foreign Office objectives. State interests were steadily entrenched, alongside the BBC itself.

In truth, that had always been the case. The highest priority users of broadcast spectrum were state institutions – defence, navigation, emergency services. There are commentators who point to the role played by the armed services and the Post Office in initially allocating spectrum. They note the convenience in terms of monitoring potential subversion of having just one broadcast licensee, and also of requiring receiving households to have licences – which was certainly not a technical necessity, nor, when broadcasting started, the only way of funding the service.

So although the BBC's monopoly status was nowhere officially enshrined, and the Post Office could always license another broadcaster, in practice there was little likelihood of this: monopoly was the preferred political and administrative outcome. In 1935, the Selsdon Committee, almost without thinking, allocated television to the BBC, as well as radio. In 1936, the Ullswater Committee – chaired, to Reith's disgust, by an octogenarian – renewed the BBC's Charter for another ten years. It also responded to a plea from the BBC's General Advisory Council, signed by Beveridge amongst others, to impose on the radio relay services used by many poorer households as an alternative to individual wireless sets, a requirement that BBC services take precedence over any others, if there were capacity limitations.

A further reflection of the close co-operation between state and broadcaster was the willingness of successive governments to support the BBC's campaign against foreign broadcasters targeting British listeners, of which the two most prominent were Radio Luxembourg and Radio Normandie. So unappealing to listeners was programming offered by the BBC on Sundays that these stations claimed to attract half as many listeners as the BBC itself. The BBC asserted such stations were pirates operating illegally – but its clear intention in campaigning against them was to block competition, not to uphold the law.

During the war, the BBC identified itself even more closely with the national interest. It also discovered that the entertainment shows on its new Forces Network were listened to by far more people than the more solemn offerings on its National Programme. After the war, these became the Light Programme and the Home Service respectively, and were joined in September 1946 by the austerely cultural Third Programme.

The change of government in 1945 challenged many old assumptions. Yet the BBC found the new administration far from hostile. Television was re-started, though resources were so scarce that tight limits were placed on capital expenditure. A White Paper promised action to "prevent the direction of commercial broadcasts to this country from abroad". There were expectations of an early and lengthy renewal of the BBC's Licence and Charter. Yet there were some worrying straws in the wind.

Sir Frederick Ogilvie, Reith's successor as BBC director-general wrote to The Times in June 1946 on the day of major Lords debate on the future of broadcasting: "a monopoly of broadcasting," he insisted, "is inevitably the negation of freedom".

At the same time in the Commons, Winston Churchill himself called for renewal of the BBC's Charter to be submitted to a joint select committee of both houses, and found over 200 MPs signing his motion to that effect. Churchill's close ally, the wartime Minister of Information Brendan Bracken, warned against "perpetuating a monopoly which will cramp the great potentialities of broadcasting".

Under growing pressure, the Labour Government that had announced it would renew the Charter for ten years without any inquiry, now conceded a five-year extension only, with an inquiry at an unspecified date. Three years later – during which time the BBC's monopoly could have been confirmed with little opposition – the Beveridge Committee was finally appointed. This cut deeply into the subsequent room for manoeuvre by both the BBC and the government, with far-reaching consequences.

Beveridge prided himself on chairing the first "thorough" inquiry into broadcasting. Sykes, Crawford, Selsdon and Ullswater spent on average just six months between appointment and report. Their total cost was less than £1,500. The Beveridge Report took 18 months from appointment to publication, and cost over £15,000. The Committee met 62 times, and received 368 submissions.

Of all the evidence Beveridge received, 40% came from the BBC. Far from having modified its ambitions or attitudes after Reith's departure in 1938, the BBC of the late 1940s was a supremely self-confident organisation. It broadcast 37 hours a day of radio on its three services, and 4 hours of television. It enjoyed wide popular support and an income of over ten million pounds a year. The Radio Times sold eight million copies a week.

The Third Programme perhaps epitomised the BBC's lofty idealism. It attracted just 1% of radio listening. It was designed, said the BBC, "to broadcast, without regard to length or difficulty, the masterpieces of music, art and letters". Even Reith, in his own evidence to Beveridge, thought that the Third Programme was "a waste of a precious wavelength", because "much of its matter is too limited in appeal". Beveridge remarked waspishly that "the Third Programme, since it began, has lost numbers of audience rather than gained them". Mischievously, he noted that although "the Charter lists the purposes of broadcasting in order as information, education and entertainment, the vast majority of listeners put these purposes in a different order, with entertainment first".

The BBC was dismissive of populism. For its first fifteen years, it turned its back on regular audience research, and it told Beveridge of the cardinal principle that research must be a servant and never the master of broadcasting. "Even if it revealed that a majority of the public were opposed to a policy which was being pursued by the BBC in a particular matter, or disliked a series of broadcasts which was on the air, that would not in itself be considered a valid reason why the policy should be reversed or the programmes withdrawn".

A decade later, the Pilkington Committee would plunge happily into the argument over whether broadcasters should provide what audiences wanted or what was good for them. The more cautious Beveridge contented himself with the Reithian dictum that programmes should be designed "not to meet but to antedate the popular vote".

The BBC's director-general at this time, Sir William Haley, had a much grander vision, of radio serving a pyramid of taste aspiring ever upwards. In evidence to Beveridge, the BBC stated its conviction "that only within the framework of three alternative programmes can its ideal of a public service of broadcasting be realised. It is an essential part of the aim to encourage listeners to move freely within the framework of the three services so that an interest first aroused in the one can be followed up and more fully satisfied in another. Only so can the level of taste be raised. If the public service of broadcasting is to be effective, it must remain a monopoly".

For Reith it boiled down to a simple assertion: only "the brute force of monopoly" could deliver the BBC's social purpose. This was the phrase that set Selwyn Lloyd's teeth on edge – "I am not attracted to the idea of compulsory uplift achieved by the brute force of monopoly". Selwyn Lloyd was not alone in finding the manipulative model of broadcasting unattractive.

For instance, Beveridge claimed not to understand the attempts to thwart foreign radio stations, indulge as they might in "giving betting news and football pool results", which he regarded as even less desirable than commercial broadcasts. He noted that Radio Luxembourg forbade jokes about the Royal Family and Members of Parliament, and failed to comment on the BBC's claim that such stations were pirates.

Moreover, said Beveridge, "most of us are opposed" to the BBC's new bid to force 4-channel radio relay stations to carry all three BBC services. Although he had shown his own colours on this issue to the Ullswater Committee, he generously summarised the majority view: "It is not certain that a listener who on grounds of reception or to suit his own personal convenience prefers the relay system should be tied down even as much as he is now to the BBC programmes, and we see no reason for making this limitation closer".

Beveridge did nearly all his own drafting, indulging himself with obscure criticisms of the BBC's failure to consult the right experts in its coverage of the Wordsworth Centenary – he meant, of course, himself! He speculated on whether the BBC's powerful commitment to Christianity was in breach of the requirement for impartiality on controversial matters. He even whimsically wondered whether the BBC was "it" or "they" – "we have to determine".

He chided the BBC for claiming that all the pre-war committees of inquiry had supported the BBC monopoly – pointing out that Sykes had opposed in principle and Ullswater had never addressed the issue, though conceding the argument in practice. But he also acknowledged that the largest of the fundamental issues his Committee faced was indeed "the Issue of Monopoly", capital I, capital M.

At the very heart of the Beveridge Report is the 8-page section on monopoly. The issue is also at the heart of the BBC's evidence. The debate covered three key areas. Whether the BBC was too large and dominating, inhibiting creative freedom and regional voices. Whether the BBC was too slow to develop television, which should be freed from the dead hand of radio. And whether monopoly was wrong in principle in a democratic society.

Surprisingly, the witnesses who opposed monopoly were few in number. They were also remarkably thin in their arguments. Advertisers were divided as to the merits of commercial broadcasting, as were even the advertising agencies. Indeed, most agencies would have been happy to leave broadcasting to the BBC, provided it accepted advertisements. The two most elaborate submissions came from the Liberal Research Group, partly supported by the Fabians, and from a pair of political commentators, Geoffrey Crowther and Robert Watson-Watt.

The Liberals described the BBC as probably "the biggest single bureaucracy in the world concerned with the propagation of ideas". Like the Fabians, the Liberals opposed monopoly in principle, but held back from proposing full-scale competitive commercial broadcasting. Their preferred solution was to leave radio untouched but to finance television in part by allowing carefully-controlled sponsorship.

Crowther and Watson-Watt developed a proposal that Crowther had first advanced in The Economist during the war: "the only ultimate safeguard of liberty lies in diversity". Because they opposed commercial funding of broadcasting, they proposed dividing the BBC into three corporations, adding the curious notion that the licence fee be divided into four, with each mini-corporation taking a quarter, and the most successful receiving the balance.

The BBC found this easy meat: "there is no need to ask whether (the bonus) would be voted to the corporation providing the most worthwhile broadcasting or to that giving the best forecasts for football pools". And the BBC went on to oppose sponsored programming, the separation of television – indeed, any breach in the edifice of monopoly.

Not surprisingly, the BBC cited Gresham's Law: "The good, in the long run, will inescapably be driven out by the bad". Indeed, any element of competition, commercial or otherwise, must be resisted: in the inevitable "fight for the greatest possible number of listeners, it would be the lower forms of mass appetite which would be more and more catered for in programmes...This is not merely a matter of BBC versus commercial broadcasting. Even if there were a number of public service corporations they would all be similarly and involuntarily driven down".

It was not just competition the BBC abhorred, but any element of commercialism. "All experience," said the BBC, "is against the belief that sponsoring has any interest in covering the whole programme field". Moreover, if any broadcaster is funded by sponsorship, it "would tend inevitably to have an adverse effect on the programme standards of the public service". Even "the incursion of the film industry into television production would be contrary to the long-term interest of the public". Competition between unfettered commercial interests and a public service corporation with obligations would "not be fair competition".

The BBC – presaging an issue that would still be open forty years later – warned that "big fights would be staged before a comparatively small audience paying 'ring-side' prices and televised to a group of cinemas paying an exclusive price for the television rights". Such damaging pursuit of exclusivity was actually attempted, noted the BBC, "in the case of the newsreels for the Olympic Games" in 1948.

"If the public service of broadcasting is to be effective," concluded the BBC, "it must remain a monopoly...It is vital to the public interest that the monopoly of both sound and television broadcasting be preserved", so as to protect impartiality, standards, regard for values, education, the arts, the raising of public taste, true citizenship and the leading of a full life. Only good health seems to have been left off the list.

In the end, it was one of the Beveridge Committee's own members, Selwyn Lloyd, who most cogently put the argument against monopoly control of such a powerful means of communication: "I cannot agree that it is in the public interest that all this actual and potential influence should be invested in a private or public monopoly...the only effective safeguard is competition from independent sources. Without that competition the basic evils and dangers of monopoly will remain".

Selwyn Lloyd concentrated on the BBC's sheer size – it had grown from 2,500 employees at the time of Ullswater in 1935 to nearly 12,000 in 1950. For all workers in broadcasting to have just one employer, and for that employer to have such excessive power, struck him as "the negation of freedom and democracy". He was also critical of the BBC's slow development of both VHF radio and television. With committee colleagues, he had visited America, and observed that New Yorkers had access to 45 radio channels and 7 television ones.

Selwyn Lloyd was content to retain a public service network: but he set it within a radical new structure. He wanted a broadcasting commission to set overall standards and rules. The licence-funded BBC could continue in radio, but he wanted additional national radio stations that could accept advertisements, as well as local stations. Television would come under a separate corporation, the BTC, with permission to accept advertisements. When frequencies became available, competitive channels could be created, allowing the BTC to revert to licence-fee funding if so desired.

He concluded that

> the present time, when television is young and VHF broadcasting has not begun, is the most suitable for a change. If the opportunity is not taken now, and if it should recur, the task of breaking the monopoly will be many times more difficult.

To our present eyes, the Selwyn Lloyd model looks both familiar and uncontroversial. For seven of his colleagues, however, it was a recipe for disaster. They were much influenced by a BBC witness's fears about the "frightening rate" at which talent was being swallowed by television. They concluded that "multiplying programmes will simply spread our already strained supply of talent the more thinly" – again, a familiar lament from the current debate over the rapid expansion of channels.

The seven hard-liners believed the case against what they called "sponsoring" was "overwhelming" – a "fantastic" price to pay for an "unworthy product...Judgement in favour of the BBC is so clear as to be obvious to all who examine the facts".

But it was not so obvious to Beveridge himself who, together with Lady Megan Lloyd George and Mrs Mary Stocks, submitted a separate minority note. They were willing to support spot advertisements on the BBC – as opposed to sponsored programmes – in order to fund the development of television. They saw a big difference between sponsorship – where the advertiser could directly influence programme content – and advertising spots, especially if these were broadcast in a block (which later became the practice in Germany). They cited the BBC's million pound annual revenue from the Radio Times as evidence of the Corporation's ability to live with commercial customers.

With this modest nod to heresy, Beveridge then assembled the full Committee – other than Selwyn Lloyd – behind his final conclusions on competition and monopoly. To appease his hard-liners, he offered a rhetorical Reithian flourish, urging that any competition should be in quality of service, not in pursuit of listeners. "To make broadcast programmes directly and automatically dependent on the preferences expressed by listeners would be contrary to the pursuit of the highest social purpose of broadcasting, which in the last resort is one of education".

He then found a way of ducking the principled issue by reference to the physical limitations on broadcast spectrum. He confidently asserted that technical advances would not "open the prospect, in any near future if ever, of free and open competition of broadcasting stations". And he offered a similarly pragmatic response to the main critics of monopoly who urged a division of the existing Corporation. He simply pointed out that the increased cost of such separation delivered too few advantages to be justified. Moreover, if there were dangers in the monopolistic control of scarce spectrum, safeguards could more readily and consistently be installed in a single corporation than in several.

The narrow ground on which he constructed his fudge put a strain on the Report's language. Despite his personal views on advertising, he faithfully reflected the majority view in arguing that sponsorship should never be allowed to take over the main financing of broadcasting – "if the people of any country want broadcasting for its own sake they must be prepared to pay for it".

At the same time, although ten of the Committee's eleven members rejected "as a guiding principle in broadcasting competition for numbers of listeners", Beveridge called in evidence the example of universities to conclude: "We do not accept that the only alternative to monopoly is degrading competition for listeners and that in broadcasting a monopoly alone can have high standards and social purpose". Having persuaded his hard-liners to accept such a formulation, Beveridge can at least be credited with creating the intellectual groundwork for the regulated form of commercial broadcasting that eventually emerged.

But such a concept was not on the agenda in 1950, except for Selwyn Lloyd. Instead, Beveridge concentrated on the short-term justification of the BBC's de facto monopoly and funding arrangements. Within that context, the prime issue was how to constrain the power of the BBC hierarchy.

For Beveridge, the main safeguard against the dangers of monopoly lay in an elaborate scheme for devolving power within the BBC to the regions. In addition, he wanted a means for the BBC Governors to by-pass the board of management and find out directly what the public thought of the BBC. He also urged a regular five-yearly review of the BBC's operations. These were the means for the Committee to answer its own question: "Can we without direct Parliamentary control prevent a chartered monopoly for broadcasting from becoming an uncontrolled bureaucracy?"

All these proposals ran into opposition from the BBC – not surprisingly, given that they challenged the tight centrist control and independence from the Governors that BBC management had built up over nearly thirty years. Even the most token of criticisms from Beveridge – that the BBC might at long last appoint a separate Director of Television to the board of management – was only grudgingly conceded. Yet these issues of devolved power came to have crucial tactical significance.

Indeed, the BBC's chairman, Lord Simon, laid the blame for the failure by the Labour government to implement Beveridge's main finding that the BBC's Charter be renewed on the dispute over Beveridge's recommendation for broadcasting commissions in Scotland, Wales and Northern Ireland.

The truth is that by 1951, Labour – already weakened in the previous year's election – was on its last legs, and broadcasting was a low priority. Stafford Cripps had resigned in October 1950, there were major parliamentary defeats over iron and steel, and Nye Bevan led a revolt against the new Chancellor's imposition of prescription charges. Prime Minister Attlee was laid low for five weeks by a duodenal ulcer, and ill-health finally forced Ernie Bevin to relinquish the Foreign Office to his old rival Herbert Morrison in March 1951. For a month, Bevin himself was dealing with broadcasting matters, as Lord Privy Seal, before he died in April 1951. His replacement as spokesman, the much more junior Patrick

Gordon-Walker, was pre-occupied as Commonwealth Secretary by the Seretse Khama affair.

Belatedly, in July, the government issued a White Paper in response to Beveridge, floating a notion – deeply unwelcome to the BBC – of local councillors sitting on the proposed broadcasting commissions. If the BBC had swallowed the Beveridge Report whole immediately on publication, perhaps its Charter could have been renewed promptly and with little opposition. Now it was all too hard, and the government had lost both interest and will. As late as August 1951, the BBC's director-general appealed to Gordon-Walker in vain for renewal. In September, the election was announced. In October, Labour were out.

Meanwhile, the BBC had made a crucial tactical error. During the Beveridge hearings, the BBC had been somewhat unfairly criticised for dragging its feet in developing television. In fact, government restrictions on capital expenditure had limited what the BBC could do. The BBC argued to Beveridge that it was devoting 20% of its resources to television, even though just 3% of its revenue came from television licences. Beveridge disapproved of this subsidy, on grounds of social equity: "those destined to remain for a long period or indefinitely outside the range of television ought not in our view be required to pay for it" – an interesting comment in the light of the BBC's later investment in BBC2 and current investment in new digital channels.

Beveridge even proposed that "advances" from radio to television be repaid in due course. But the biggest single point of pressure was that television lacked a director, and was only represented on the board of management through the home broadcasting directorate. In October 1950, whilst the Beveridge Report was still being drafted, the BBC belatedly appointed a Director of Television, but chose to pass over the obvious candidate, Norman Collins, the Controller of Television, because he was not seen as board-of-management material. Instead, the job went to George Barnes, who luxuriated in the titles of Controller of the Third

Programme and Director of the Spoken Word. Such was the BBC in 1950.

Collins promptly resigned, and became the most important single figure in the ensuing three-year campaign to end the BBC's monopoly. The BBC's chairman, Lord Simon, was to concede that "if we hadn't fired Collins there would be no commercial television now" – curiously forgetting that Collins had not actually been fired. He later became deputy chairman of one of the first ITV franchises, ATV.

Collins linked up with two groups – commercial interests in the shape of the advertising and TV set manufacturing industries, and a dedicated group of backbench Conservative MPs who had taken over the principled argument set out by Selwyn Lloyd. This group had been greatly strengthened by the two elections that had brought over a hundred new Conservatives into the Commons. The most prominent of these were John Rodgers, with strong advertising connections, Ian Orr-Ewing, whose business interests embraced TV set manufacture, and John Profumo, who became chairman of the influential Broadcasting Study Group of Conservative MPs, created in 1951. The group's secretary was Mark Chapman-Walker, who, remarkably, doubled as chief propagandist at Conservative Central Office under the chairmanship of Lord Woolton, who served as Churchill's cabinet fixer. Chapman-Walker was another future deputy chairman of an ITV franchise.

The Conservatives had won the election without any mention of broadcasting in their manifesto. Only three cabinet members favoured a commercial system. The new Postmaster General announced a short-term extension of the BBC Charter. Then party battle commenced.

Support for the BBC and public service broadcasting was strong, so the insurgents – who were always a minority in their party – concentrated on a sponsored television service as an addition to the BBC's provision, initially using the BBC's own transmitters

40 during their down time. Their tactic worked. Woolton calculated that the supporters of the BBC he had to placate would be content with a compromise that protected the BBC's monopoly in radio – which, after all, was the dominant medium – but allowed competition in television. That was the position announced in his White Paper of May 1952.

He was greeted, at least in the House of Lords, with howls of rage. Lord Radcliffe – who by now had rejoined the BBC's General Advisory Council as chairman – described commercial television as "too dangerous a hazard" to risk. Lord Hailsham saw the White Paper as a betrayal of the BBC and of the purpose of broadcasting. Lord Reith famously fulminated that someone had introduced Christianity into England, "and somebody introduced smallpox, bubonic plague and the Black Death. Somebody is now minded to introduce sponsored broadcasting".

The General Advisory Council had met the day before the debate for what Lord Brabazon, a consistent critic of monopoly, called a "pep talk" from the BBC's director-general and the chairman. Seventeen peers spoke in opposition to the government. More than half were closely connected with the BBC.

The government retreated, with its spokesmen in both houses suggesting that any form of competition was some years away. But perhaps the most significant development of that month was Patrick Gordon-Walker's response to the further renewal of the BBC's Charter and Licence. He committed the Labour Party to restoring monopoly if the Conservatives pressed ahead with introducing competition – a pledge repeated by his party leader the following year. This made it virtually impossible for any pro-BBC majority in the Commons to emerge, as it might have done on a free vote. The decisive debate would now be within the Conservative Party, whose whips would impose the outcome.

The final battle was fought through 1953. Christopher Mayhew, a Labour MP and experienced broadcaster, strongly committed to the BBC's cause, created the National Television Council, aided by such luminaries as Lord Simon and Lady Violet Bonham Carter. The Council's inauguration was announced in *The Times* – now edited by former BBC director-general Sir William Haley – in June 1952, immediately after the coronation, which for the first time had seen the television audience outnumbering that for radio.

Just as significantly, the BBC's triumphant coverage had been re-transmitted in the United States, often with advertising interspersed, despite agreements with the BBC to the contrary. One broadcaster, NBC, even used a chimpanzee called J Fred Muggs on air, much to Mayhew's glee. Within a month came the latest announcement of government plans, containing the feeble commitment that "competitive television might be permitted to operate". The *Daily Express* promptly proclaimed that "commercial television died yesterday".

The *Express*, like most newspapers with the exception of the *Daily Mirror*, was vocal in its hostility to commercial television. Other open critics included cinema and theatre interests, such as Granada, ABC (Associated British Corporation) and the major unions, NATKE (National Association of Theatrical Television and Kine) and what later became the ACTT (Association of Cinematograph Television and Allied Technicians). All of these opponents were, of course, soon to be greatly enriched by the breaking of the BBC monopoly.

The commercial lobby fought back, with the advertisers and Conservative Central Office setting up a Popular Television Association, which managed to attract such supporters as the historian AJP Taylor, the journalist Malcolm Muggeridge and the cricketer Alec Bedser.

Finally, the deal was done. Party managers headed off potential revolts in the Lords by imposing a regulator on the new commercial system with enough public funding to build a separate transmission network, and by restricting advertising to spots, not sponsors – just as Beveridge's own minority report had proposed.

The Conservative backbench group was horrified. The last thing they had wanted was a kind of junior BBC, as they termed the future regulatory body. But the tactic worked, with only 87 peers voting against the plan, despite Lord Hailsham's impassioned attack on what he described as "a shabby and squalid constitutional error" in betraying the BBC without putting the issue to the electorate in the form of a manifesto pledge.

In July 1954, the Independent Television Act was passed, and in September 1955, ITV was launched to just 370,000 homes whose television sets were capable of receiving the new service. By contrast, eight million people listened that night to BBC radio's most popular serial to hear its lead character, Grace Archer, die in a fire. This burnt sacrifice – designed months in advance as a stunt to divert attention from ITV's first night – seemed to fulfil the BBC's own gloomy prognostications about the negative effects of competition.

Did the Beveridge Report also perish in the blaze? In just over three years, the changes in the political climate had been so sharp that they left the Report's main conclusions in their wake. As austerity gave way to modest affluence, Conservative instincts more accurately reflected the public mood.

By contrast, Beveridge was a creature of its time, trapped in the constricted assumptions of the 1940s, just as Britain was emerging from its pre-war shell. With our fifty years of hindsight, we might even identify as Beveridge's biggest omission the failure to switch – as urged by the likes of Lord Brabazon – from a 405-line system to a 625-line system at an opportunely early moment. A generation of consumers paid the price for that lack of vision.

Even so, Beveridge was a seminal moment in the development of the political structure of British broadcasting. The Report focused the argument over monopoly for the first time. It was published just as television emerged from the shadows of radio – and even that wily fox Lord Woolton failed to register television's true significance. It exposed issues of the BBC's governance that remain unresolved today, as the debate over the Scottish Six O'clock News demonstrates.

More importantly, it set the tone and the framework for all the reports that succeeded it, for ill or for good. Even if the answers it provided were rejected, it offered confirmation that an orderly and regulated structure for broadcasting could be created by the political process. And within five years of ITV's launch, another committee of inquiry would be set up which effectively concluded that Beveridge had been right all along. Pilkington's scathing indictment of ITV is the subject of the next lecture.

[2]
Pilkington

25 February 1999

At the beginning of 1951, when the Beveridge Report on the future of broadcasting was published, 85% of UK households held BBC licences. The number of sound-only licences was 11.68 million, whilst combined radio and television licences amounted to less than 600,000. A decade later, 95% of UK households possessed BBC licences, but the proportions had been dramatically reversed. In 1961, the level of combined licences was 11.66 million, whilst sound-only licences numbered just 3.66 million.

The broadcasting world had been transformed by a twin revolution. In the words of the 1962 Pilkington Report, television that had taken over the "compulsive element" from radio. But just as the balance of power and spending within the BBC thereby shifted, so the introduction of commercial television in 1955 changed broadcasting irrevocably. The last opportunity to forestall ITV had passed when the Labour Party lost the 1955 election. By the time of the 1959 election, Labour's leader, Hugh Gaitskell, had reluctantly conceded: "commercial television has come to stay".

46 ITV had survived a problematic birth. On its first night, fewer than 5% of homes with televisions could see the infant service. BBC Television scheduled *The Donald Duck Story* against ITV's opening night coverage of its own white-tie launch banquet at the Guildhall. The BBC's burnt sacrifice of Grace Archer – to the horror of a radio audience that dwarfed any for a television programme that night – smacked a little of overkill.

Yet within weeks, those homes equipped with both television services showed overwhelming preference for the newcomer. As the BBC's Head of Audience Research painstakingly explained to the Governors the elementary principles of competitive scheduling – such as regular weekly series – ITV swiftly introduced *Double Your Money, I Love Lucy, Sunday Night At The London Palladium, Dragnet, Take Your Pick* and *Robin Hood*. In dual-channel homes, ITV rapidly captured more than 60% of viewing, and all ten top places in the weekly list of most-watched programmes.

A BBC relay of a performance of *La Boheme* managed to secure just 2% of dual-channel viewers against ITV's Val Parnell's *Star Night*. Along with hundreds of trained personnel, the BBC also started losing programmes to ITV – of which the first was *Muffin the Mule*. But even these successes for ITV, coupled with the rapid spread of its transmitters and coverage, could not disguise the early financial losses suffered by the pioneering commercial contractors appointed by the Independent Television Authority, the ITA.

Within six months, the biggest company, Associated-Rediffusion, was facing a cumulative deficit of nearly £5 million. One of its shareholders, Associated Newspapers, sold most of its stake to its partner, Rediffusion, at a heavy discount. Rediffusion took one of their own programme titles literally, doubling their stake in ITV by secretly underwriting the losses of Granada Television for its first four years.

ITV's regulator, the ITA, had planned to create competitive franchises in each transmission area. Shortage of frequencies prevented this, so the ITA carved up the days of the week between contractors in different areas, so as to generate competition and diversity. The ITV companies responded with a carve-up of their own. To reduce the financial pressure on them, they persuaded the ITA to tolerate a system of cost-sharing whereby all the programmes the largest four companies produced were transmitted across the whole network at pre-agreed prices.

Also, seizing the moment of greatest perceived financial danger, ITV evicted from peak-time much of the serious programming to which it was committed. In February 1956, 90 minutes of *Hamlet* had managed to push a BBC programme – *What's My Line* – into the Top Ten for the first time in five months. It was not a mistake ITV intended to repeat.

The turning point came in mid-1956, as it became clear that advertisers judged ITV a success and started voting with their wallets. By the time the contractor for Central Scotland launched, its proprietor, Canadian newspaperman Roy Thomson, could describe his ITV station as "a licence to print your own money".

By 1958, when the BBC was spending just £14 million on television, ITV's revenue was nearly £50 million. The profit margin was 60% of revenue. At ATV, where Norman Collins, former BBC Controller of Television was now ensconced, the shares had multiplied in value 220 times in just three years. Collins – in Asa Briggs' memorable phrase, now one of the BBC's "most intelligent, talented, determined and deeply detested adversaries" – had extracted a rich revenge. But the power of television, the level of profits, and the publication of a book – Professor Wilson's *Pressure Group* – demonstrating how a well-organised minority in the Conservative Party had squeezed ITV into existence, all combined to invite the inevitable backlash.

The first set of ITV contracts was due to expire in 1964. The BBC's Charter was extended by two years to match this expiry date – a decision that seemed to beg the creation of a successor

48 committee to Beveridge. However, Prime Minister Harold Macmillan was reluctant to take that step ahead of the 1959 election, and it took some pressure from his Postmaster General Reginald Bevins before an announcement was finally made to the Commons in July 1960.

Bizarrely, one of the three names considered by Macmillan for chairmanship of the committee was Lord Radcliffe, who had been forced to stand down in favour of Lord Beveridge in 1949. In the end, the choice fell on the glass manufacturer, Sir Harry Pilkington, who had just completed a three-year stint chairing a Royal Commission on the pay of doctors and dentists.

In September, the committee's membership was announced. There were no politicians – the practice of appointing MPs of all parties to such committees had died out in the 1950s. Instead, the emphasis was on trade unionists, women, and representatives of Scotland, Wales and Northern Ireland. There were gestures to popular taste, with the inclusion of the former England soccer captain, Billy Wright, and the comedienne Joyce Grenfell. Two of the more imaginative appointees – industrialist Sir Jock Campbell and theatre director Peter Hall – resigned fairly swiftly. But the name that came to be associated most closely with the Pilkington Report – more so even than its chairman – was Richard Hoggart: educationist, socialist, and author of the immensely influential study of the roots of working class culture, *The Uses Of Literacy*.

Hoggart became best known to the wider public as a defence witness in the trial of Penguin Books over the publication in paperback of *Lady Chatterley's Lover*. His combination of earthiness, eloquence and high moral tone undoubtedly strongly influenced the Pilkington Report's language and conclusions. Hoggart's starting position could be gauged by an article he had published early in 1960, in which he described ITV's programmes as looking "nicely acceptable – but whose texture is as little that of a good life as processed bread is like home-made bread". That Hoggart found a soulmate in the Committee's secretary, Dennis Lawrence, ensured that the Report would be imbued throughout with an earnestness that many of its readers found instantly repellent.

The Pilkington Report took 23 months from announcement to publication. It received 852 submissions in all, and met 78 times. Its cost, at £45,000, was three times that of Beveridge – as much a measure of inflation as of multiplication of work. Its number of recommendations, at 120, showed a more modest advance on Beveridge's 100.

Pilkington's terms of reference were to consider the future – and financing – of broadcasting and of the bodies providing it within the UK, namely the ITA and the BBC. This effectively ensured the future of these organisations, which was perhaps just as well, given the ominous tone of the Report's third paragraph, which noted with seeming regret that our "terms of reference preclude us from recommending that broadcasting should again be a monopoly".

If Pilkington stopped short of such a draconian step, he nonetheless put forward – in his 43rd recommendation – a succinct proposal for the radical overhaul of ITV. If implemented, in the view of Bevins, it would have "destroyed commercial television". That this core proposal failed to find political favour did not, however, mean that the Report could be dismissed, in the way Beveridge was by some, as an irrelevance. Many of Pilkington's recommendations were implemented, with important consequences – the creation of BBC2, the switch to colour, the change from 405-line transmission to 625-line, the allocation of local radio to the BBC, the rejection of subscription television, the continuation of the licence fee and the delay in using the fourth channel.

Just as importantly, the spirit of recommendation 43 proved remarkably resilient. Its influence on the final shaping of Channel 4 may not be obvious to most commentators, especially as two decades were to pass between Pilkington's publication and Channel 4's launch; but it was real. And Pilkington's language, however out of tune with our present prejudices, strikes a distinctive note which is instantly recognisable, even 37 years after first reading.

Pilkington very self-consciously placed himself in the tradition of committees of inquiry. "Since 1923, new and impending developments have from time to time required a fresh examination of the principles of broadcasting by a succession of independent committees. As a Committee, we take our place in the succession". Indeed, when recommending extending the BBC's Charter and the life of the ITA for a further twelve years, Pilkington was calculating the timing of his successor's appointment.

But in one crucial respect, Pilkington inflicted serious damage on the credibility of the committee-of-inquiry system. He took the submissions from witnesses as objective evidence. Worse still, he disingenuously attributed his findings to the evidence submitted. The Report claimed to have started with "no general doctrine, no pre-conceived principles": "our approach has...been empirical". Yet Dennis Lawrence, the Committee's secretary, had issued to its members before they met position papers which made key assumptions about the social significance of broadcasting. These underpinned the crucial third chapter of the Report, on "The Purposes of Broadcasting" – itself, curiously enough, drafted after the Committee's main recommendations had been reached, contrary to the clear impression left by the Report.

That most of the evidence Pilkington received came from self-selected groups and was inevitably subjective seemed not to have occurred to the Committee. Professor Richard Rose understandably criticised the Report because "it asserted that television is 'of profound social significance' without any empirical evidence to support so controversial a hypothesis". Pilkington did receive submissions from the social scientists Hilde Himmelweit and Hans Eysenck, but commissioned no research of its own. When it was pointed out to the Committee that people could always switch off their sets, and that it may not be "of great relevance to criticise television at all", the Report revealingly noted: "we found this last a deflating thought".

Pilkington's many conclusions flowed logically from its core presumption. "Our own judgement, after weighing such evidence as is available, leads us to a clear conclusion. It is that...unless and until there is unmistakable proof to the contrary, the presumption must be that television is and will be a main factor in influencing the values and moral standards of our society".

Three other a priori judgements underpinned Pilkington's thinking. First, the nature of broadcasting spectrum was such that "since the frequency space available to broadcasting is limited, it is essential that what is available should be used to best advantage". The Report noted that "a control which derives from the need to ensure the orderly use of scarce frequencies – and is thus technical in its purpose – is applied here for reasons which are essentially social".

Secondly, in the belief that broadcasting "should not be left to the ordinary processes of commercial enterprise" nor "undertaken by the state", Pilkington warmly endorsed the public corporation model. To complete the central structure of the argument, Pilkington simply asserted that "the duty of the public corporations has been, and remains, to bring to public awareness the whole range of worthwhile, significant activity and experience".

Upon this base of non-sequential arguments, Pilkington mounted a formidable array of definitions of good broadcasting and how it was to be achieved. "Broadcasting", he believed, "must be in a constant and sensitive relationship with the moral condition of society". But there was no automatic path to virtue. "Broadcasting", said the Report, "is more nearly an art than a science... no written formula for good broadcasting is possible. Good broadcasting is a practice, not a prescription".

Pilkington had no doubt as to how to test the merits of the BBC and the ITA – by what they did rather than by what they said. "Broadcasting should be judged not by the stated aims of the broadcasters, but by their achievements; and it is in the light of these achievements that the structure of their organisations should be examined. We have considered first the product and then the producer".

In a more ominous note for the ITA, Pilkington continued: "we thought it right to set our standards high. It is not enough that the broadcasters should nearly achieve the purposes of broadcasting, or that one should achieve them and not another".

If one phrase has come to be associated with the Pilkington Report over the decades, it is "patronising and arrogant". Curiously, the phrase itself is the Report's own, at the heart of a remarkable disquisition on one of the oldest chestnuts mulled over by writers on broadcasting – should the broadcasters give the public what they want or what is good for them? This is, of course, a false dichotomy, presuming that the audience is an undifferentiated mass. For Pilkington, it proved a trap all the more dangerous for the Committee's false belief that they had escaped its snares.

Pilkington found the phrase "to give the public what it wants" offensive and misleading: "It has the appearance of an appeal to democratic principle but the appearance is deceptive. It is in fact patronising and arrogant. We reject it utterly...what the public wants and what it has the right to get is the freedom to choose from the widest range of programme matter. Anything less than that is deprivation".

The Report cited with approval one of its witnesses: "those who say they give the public what it wants begin by underestimating public taste, and end by debauching it".

Pilkington equally rejected as "patronising and arrogant" the notion of giving the public what you think is good for it. "The possible range of subject matter is inexhaustible...so the broadcaster must explore it and choose from it first. This might be called 'giving a lead': but it is not the lead of the autocratic and arrogant. It is the proper exercise of responsibility by public authorities duly constituted as trustees for the public interest".

But Pilkington did not content himself with these even-handed banalities. He described the effect of seeking "the largest possible audience" and appealing to a "low level of public taste" as "to produce a passively acquiescent or even indifferent audience rather than an actively interested one". In a phrase reminiscent of Hoggart's pre-judgement about home-made bread, he remarked that "too often viewers were offered neither meat nor poison but pap".

The most sustained passage in this vein displays a mind-set reaching back to John Stuart Mill's comparison of the fool satisfied and the wise man dissatisfied. "It is by no means obvious that a vast audience watching television all the evening will derive a greater sum of enjoyment from it than will several small audiences each of which watches for part of the evening only. For the first may barely tolerate what it sees, while the second might enjoy it intensely".

The idea that the preferences of the majority might have to defer to those of minorities found its most extreme form in a quite separate section of the Report, on radio relay services. We can recall that the Beveridge Committee rejected a request from the BBC that, where listeners received their services from relay systems rather than their own radios, such systems should be required to give full precedence to the BBC's three radio channels – as a planned broadcasting unit – ahead of foreign radio channels such as Luxembourg. Beveridge could not see why the relay audience of more than a million homes should be more restricted in choice than people with the freedom to tune their own sets as they wished. Not so Pilkington.

In the case of sound radio, listeners would ideally be able to receive all the BBC sound services and foreign sound programmes. But, if they cannot, then the requirement that a public service of broadcasting must seek to satisfy the needs and aspirations of minorities as well as of majorities must prevail. To put it at its simplest: a minority must not be deprived of the Third Programme/Network Three [as Radio Three used to be called], in order to provide two light programmes (one BBC, one foreign) – even though many listeners would, more often than not, choose one or other of them. Accordingly, we recommend that the relay licence should require licensees to relay all the national sound services of the BBC before relaying foreign services.

So, forty years after the BBC's foundation, we still find the concept of producer-driven broadcasting fully in control: consumer choice must give way to a planned service of broadcasting. A group of homes dependent on a relay must pay to listen to the radio, but may not express preferences. The careless assumption that serious programming is superior to non-serious programming, and that minority tastes are superior to majority ones, fails even to acknowledge that there might be a difference between two "light" programmes, one from the BBC and one from abroad: indeed, listeners may not even choose between these two. Small wonder The Economist accused Pilkington of "compulsive nannying".

Interestingly, the BBC itself accepted that its old notion of a tightly-integrated radio service was having to become more segregated, under pressure not just from Luxembourg but from television, and from the spread of portable and car radios. Soon, the advent of pirate radio would drive the BBC even further down the road of segregated services – a trend that Pilkington deplored. But for the moment, the Committee concluded that "the BBC's sound services, in our judgement, succeed in realising the purposes of broadcasting". Indeed, the Report endorsed the BBC's claim to start local broadcasting, as part of a continuing sound monopoly: "one service, and one service only, should be planned", as recommendation 89 put it.

But radio was really a sideshow in the Pilkington Report. Television was at its heart. And again the BBC emerged with flying colours. This was no accident. The BBC had been preparing for Pilkington for some time, and the appointment of Hugh Greene as Director-General in January 1960 gave further impetus to this process. But Hugh Greene was not content with the elaborate paperwork merging from the secretariat.

He arranged a special screening of Richard Cawston's award-winning documentary, *This Is The BBC*, for the Committee. And he addressed the issue of audience share.

In his memoirs he wrote:

> However good our case may be, there would be no political or public support for any recommendations the Pilkington Committee might make along the lines we urged if people were still tuning to ITV in an overwhelming majority. Why should they pay a licence fee if they were not using the BBC? I therefore told the television service that without any abandonment of BBC standards they must aim at increasing our share of the television audience from its lowest ratio of 27:73 to 50:50 by the time the Pilkington Committee reported. That was exactly achieved at the beginning of 1963.

In fact, Pilkington had reported six months earlier, but Greene's objective had by then been largely achieved, with such programmes as *Juke Box Jury*, *The Black And White Minstrel Show*, *Six-Five Special* and *The Benny Hill Show*. Perhaps Greene's major contribution to the BBC's success in the Pilkington inquiry was to endorse the Committee's own prejudices. He considered television "one of the main factors influencing the values and moral attitudes of our society" and agreed it was the BBC's duty "to give a give a lead to public taste", even at "the risk of paternalism". By contrast, the ITA's chairman offered the view that television largely reflected society as it was – and that society would be little different in the absence of television. Pilkington found such an approach deeply irresponsible.

Amongst the BBC's minor victories with the Committee was to persuade it to maintain the restriction on broadcast hours on each channel – so constraining ITV's revenue and the BBC's costs at the same time. Pilkington also adopted the BBC's opposition to both a Broadcast Consumers' Council and subscription television.

In 1962, subscription was effectively pay-per-view television, not the monthly system developed in the last decade, so Pilkington's arguments as to the excessive cost of delivering programmes and collecting revenue have much less force today. But the main objection to subscription – borrowed from the BBC – was that it might divert key programming, like sports events, away from free television. Pilkington thought it would be wrong to use a scarce terrestrial channel for such a purpose, and that wire distribution would never have more than limited reach.

Pilkington, of course, could not resist a grander objection. Any television service, even delivered by wire, was still television, and so must be run by a public corporation and conform to "the purposes of broadcasting". As subscription television would, he argued, be driven to appeal to the majority, it could not meet those purposes, even if it was not using public frequencies. Accordingly, he recommended "that no service of subscription television be authorised", and by the same woeful logic, that no experiment be allowed as it was simply wrong in principle. In the end, an experiment was authorised – but subscription technology was too primitive at this stage for it to have any significance.

In only one area was the BBC disappointed by Pilkington: its desire for all the proceeds of the licence fee to pass automatically to it. Pilkington, instead, supported ministerial discretion, on the grounds that it was "largely through the control of finance that authority is exercised" – a formulation seemingly lacking in courage, but consistent with the Report's "from us to them" view of broadcasting.

As it turned out, ministers soon abandoned this limit on the BBC's operations, relying instead on the right to limit the licence fee itself. By contrast, Pilkington expressed his approval of "the principle on which the BBC allocates money between its services" – in other words, reserving for radio's use the proceeds from the £1 sound-only licence and from one-third of the £3 combined licence. Within a decade, of course, the radio licence had been abolished – as too inefficient to collect – and the BBC was left to decide for itself what proportion of the television licence to divert to radio.

Perhaps Greene's neatest trick in managing Pilkington was to admit that the BBC was not perfect. On the one hand, the BBC declined to withdraw a single word of its apocalyptic evidence to Beveridge about the evils of competition; on the other, it acknowledged that its light entertainment might even have improved as a result of competition. But in general, even if Pilkington "found in the BBC an all-round professionalism", it picked up from the BBC regretful hints that competition had forced it to depart from "its own ideal of public service broadcasting".

> Mr Carleton Greene told us that the BBC did not aim at acquiring a particular proportion of the total television audience [which we know from Greene's own words to be untrue]. But the Corporation had, he added, to realise that if the proportion fell too low, their claim to be the national instrument of broadcasting would be impaired.

Greene's solution was simple. The BBC should be allocated a second television channel. Pilkington quickly picked up his line of argument, which rested on the attractive notion of complementary scheduling. "The needs of the many groups of which a mass audience is composed cannot be met except by two programmes planned in contrast with each other".

In fact, the BBC had started calling for a second channel in 1954, even before ITV was launched, but the then Postmaster General, Dr Charles Hill, had turned the idea down in 1956 on economic grounds. In 1960, within weeks of becoming Director-General, Greene went public with his bid. Certainly, international frequency planning had opened up the possibility of more channels, but the first priority seemed to be the switch from 405-line transmission (a standard unique to the UK) to the European norm of 625-lines. So Pilkington, having been advised by the technical specialists that new allocations of bandwidth made room for at least four channels on 625-lines, recommended that two be used for simulcasting the existing services, and the other two for new services.

Logically, this suggested an ITV2 as well as a BBC2. Unexpectedly, the ITA recommended that the two additional services be allocated to a third, separate general service, funded by advertising, and to a specialist educational channel. This seemingly selfless proposal had a thinly-concealed sub-text. The ITA disingenuously argued that, given their pre-existing responsibility for one advertising-funded channel, they could happily supervise another. Meanwhile, the BBC's ambitions would be thwarted.

Pilkington rejected every aspect of the ITA's argument, preferring in its entirety the BBC's approach. A separate educational channel was inadvisable, as it might diminish the willingness of generalist broadcasters to include educational material. Moreover, the Committee was much drawn to the BBC's idea of complementary scheduling of two channels. The aim would be "not that either channel would be given a minority character", but "so to construct the sequence on each that viewers who did not switch would find themselves exposed at some time of the evening to informational material".

This crudely manipulative model of television was reminiscent of Sir William Haley's vision of the way the three BBC radio services could mould the audience. That this was already being overtaken by events cut no ice with Pilkington. He simply did not want another separate service: "competition in audience ratings we regard as regrettable". The recommendation for a BBC2 also coincided with the views of most witnesses that if there were an additional service, the BBC should provide it. But what of ITV2?

It did not help ITV that the ITA's founder-chairman, Sir Kenneth Clark, was amongst those who disapproved of any extension of television: he "considered that there was not the material needed to support any extension of television services". Indeed, he feared "a Gadarene descent", given the existing evidence that television could not in his view pitch too low in its appeal to public taste.

With friends like this, ITV scarcely needed enemies: but there was no lack of them amongst those giving evidence to Pilkington. Bernard Levin had long since condemned 60% of ITV's offerings as "not fit to feed to the cat". But now the pigeons came home to roost. Pilkington noted that nearly all the disquiet and dissatisfaction in the submissions it received related to television, and nearly all of that to ITV.

The adjectives used included "vapid", "puerile", "derivative", "repetitious" and "trivial". Triviality – in content, approach and presentation – was the worst sin, "a natural vice of television", "more dangerous to the soul than wickedness". That such accusations were coming from a narrow group of organisations like the TUC, the Society for Education in Film and Television, the National Union of Teachers, the Association of Education Committees and the self-appointed Council for Children's Welfare did not seem to strike Pilkington as worth noting.

Pilkington also accepted uncritically statistics presented by the Council for Children's Welfare, to the effect that ITV was showing more than twice as many westerns and crime series between 6pm and 9pm as the BBC. Only after publication could the ITA point out that its figures were almost identical to the BBC's, if innocuous material such as *Biggles*, *Flicka* and *Boyd QC* was excluded. Too late. Pilkington had concluded that "the portrayal of violence, in its amount, treatment and timing is unsatisfactory on independent television".

Another major source of criticism were quiz shows – "large rewards were to be won for little effort" in the course of a naked "appeal to fear and greed". Party game shows "humiliated members of the public". "We conclude that the dissatisfaction with television can largely be ascribed to the independent television service...[hence] the widespread opinion that much in television is trivial".

And it was not just ITV's programmes that were objectionable. "On the content of advertisements there has been much disquiet, and we believe it to be generally justified...we conclude, then, that advertisements which appeal to human weakness could well in the long run have a deplorable individual and social effect".

But Pilkington reserved his major attack for ITV's structure. If his terms of reference prevented him recommending abolition of the ITA, he was certainly free to point out that the ITV companies had no right to exist beyond 1964. As for the Authority, it had misconceived the relationship between itself and its contractors. They were not friends and partners. The idea that the ITA could rely on "persuasion and influence" to "realise the purposes of broadcasting" was, in a word, "mistaken".

In Pilkington's view, the ITA should only have chosen programme contractors who would "unfailingly" make the sale of advertising time incidental to the best possible service of broadcasting. Not having done so, the ITA lacked the means to correct the situation. "The ITA's power to control the companies...is illusory and negligible...the sanctions available to the Authority...are either derisory, or too extreme, or inappropriate...once appointed, a contractor cannot be effectively disciplined".

The Committee fully recognised that ITV's commercial success was "phenomenal". But the structural fault-line in ITV was unmistakable. "The two purposes of ITV do not coincide": making advertising time "as desirable as possible to those who want it [is] an aim largely incompatible with the purposes of broadcasting... that the companies are widely regarded as principals and the Authority as their spokesman is unsatisfactory...it must, therefore, be master and be seen to be master".

Pilkington could not disinvent commercial television. But in their 43rd recommendation, the Committee came up with an ingenious structure. The contractors would be given modest output guarantees if they chose to convert to being purely programme providers. Everything else would be done by the ITA – planning the schedule, buying the programmes, selling the airtime and passing surplus revenues to the Treasury. This would "remove the incentive always to aim at maximum audiences".

The similarity between this proposal and the eventual structure of Channel 4 will no doubt strike many people. Indeed, there are those who have noted that such an insulation of the programme-makers and schedulers from direct commercial pressures might allow the BBC to operate as an advertising-funded public broadcaster. But at the time, recommendation 43 found few takers, apart from a group of Labour MPs, led by Christopher Mayhew, by now his party's broadcasting spokesman.

Pilkington had two objectives: to reform ITV and to block ITV2 until reform took place. "We recommend that, as long as independent television is constituted and organised as at present, it should not provide any additional services of television". Even if re-organisation took place, there should not be an ITV2 for at least five years thereafter.

Even before the Pilkington Report was published, Bevins was alerting the cabinet to its deficiencies: "this verdict is unbalanced and unfair. I think the Committee have been swayed unduly by the evidence of prejudiced but articulate organisations". The ITA's chairman protested direct to the Home Secretary, Rab Butler: "the Report is loaded with prejudice and abounds with misrepresentation and distortion". One ITV company chairman burned an effigy of Sir Harry and his report on a huge bonfire. Some MPs used the phrase "moral authoritarianism".

The sharpest criticism was of recommendation 43. The Sunday Times – long before its present proprietor owned it – described the attempt "to make the ITA into another BBC" as "the hopeless last resort of men who fundamentally fear the operation of a free society". Less hysterical, but no less damning, was the verdict of the eminent television critic, Peter Black. "The Pilkington Report thought that reform could be achieved by creating a service that was supported by advertising but not dependent on popular appeal. It is an attractive notion to those who dislike advertising and popular appeal".

Of course, others were less critical. Beveridge called Pilkington to say he entirely agreed with the contents of the Report. By this time, Beveridge was suffering from selective memory. He told the House of Lords that he had changed his mind about preserving the BBC's monopoly, but was opposed to advertisements – forgetting that he had actually supported advertising on the BBC in 1951, but expressed reservations about monopoly. The next rung down, former director-general Sir William Haley congratulated Greene on a splendid vindication for the BBC. As Bevins himself joked, Pilkington had found the BBC "whiter than white" – quoting an advertising slogan of the day.

But Bevins was no longer in control of the outcome. As a minister outside cabinet, he lacked clout. It was Butler, the Home Secretary, who led the cabinet committee that decided how to implement the Report. BBC2 was swiftly endorsed, and came on air 21 months later. A new Television Act was submitted to a Parliament which had little appetite for a re-run of the passionate post-Beveridge debates. As one Labour spokesman put it, "we have left behind the old battle". Even Patrick Gordon-Walker, who had vowed to abolish ITV, now conceded that "competition has done some good". Christopher Mayhew chose to resign as a front-bench spokesman on broadcasting when he failed to persuade his colleagues to support recommendation 43 – though his party conference later that year unanimously endorsed it.

Yet the Television Act of 1964 shifted the balance of power significantly in ITV. The ITA now had much greater control over the schedule, even if the companies remained in place. There was an explicit requirement for high standards, proper balance, a "wide showing for programmes of merit" and "a sufficient amount of time" for news. It may only have been of symbolic importance, but the 1954 formulation of "entertainment, instruction and information" became in 1964 language "information, education and entertainment", echoing the BBC Charter.

Of equal significance was the pre-emptive strike by the Conservative government the year before Pilkington reported, when Chancellor Selwyn Lloyd introduced a Television Advertising Duty, designed to reduce the excessive profits of the ITV companies. Recalling his role in the creation of ITV, Selwyn Lloyd expressed the hope that the companies would "not mind being bitten by the hand that had fed them". In the 1964 Act, this Duty was replaced by the first version of the ITV levy – and again, the ITA fought a losing battle, with a turnover levy being enacted rather than the profits levy it preferred. This was expected to siphon off more than half of ITV's profitability.

For ITV, the outcome of the Pilkington process was deeply painful. The official history of ITV ascribed the defeat to the programming cuts made in early 1956 and an unwillingness to make dutiful noises: "through a combination of parsimony and stubborn devotion to the concept of people's television, ITV missed an opportunity to acquire easy merit in the eyes of the Committee". Hugh Greene was more dismissive of the companies: "they were lazy in the public presentation of their case and fatally casual, even, I believe, contemptuous, in the presentation of their evidence. They got what was coming to them".

The change in the ITV system led Norman Collins to threaten that no contractor would renew its licence in 1964. But his day had passed. All the companies duly re-applied, and the largest – Associated-Rediffusion, the most buccaneering of the pioneers – was reduced to a junior partner in the London franchise when the re-invigorated ITA eventually came to make its judgements. The new chairman, Dr Hill – now ennobled after being fired from Macmillan's cabinet – was determined to make his mark.

The Pilkington Committee may have sailed upon a tide of anti-ITV feeling, but its Report decisively focused that feeling and triggered the reforms of the 1964 Act. The deficiencies of a system of excessive ITA discretion were not resolved for a further thirty years – but that can hardly be held against Pilkington, whose own, more radical, proposals would not bear fruit until Channel 4 was born.

That process took its first tentative steps in the final parliamentary debate of 1963, when Bevins expressed the hope "to issue a licence for ITA2 during 1965", in time to "come on air in 1966". Within a year, Bevins and the Tory government were history. How ITV2 came to join them there is the subject of the next lecture.

[3]
Annan

2 March 1999

In May 1970, the Minister for Posts and Telecommunications – as the Postmaster General had been grandly re-titled by Harold Wilson – summoned a distinguished liberal academic to his office for a glass of brandy. The academic, Lord Annan, Provost of University College, London and previously Provost of King's College, Cambridge, was invited to chair a new inquiry into the future of broadcasting. Of course, said the minister, in that future, television as we knew it might well disappear, to be replaced by new technological marvels.

Actually, it was the minister who disappeared. John Stonehouse soon thereafter faked his own death by drowning, re-surfaced in Australia, and six years later faced 18 charges of fraud, false pretences and forgery at the Old Bailey.

The Annan Inquiry followed a course a little – but only a little – less eventful. To give Stonehouse due credit, his decision to appoint Annan had required his overcoming resistance from his own Prime Minister as well as from the BBC and the ITV, none of whom thought another full-scale investigation necessary less than eight years after Pilkington had reported.

The ministry was looking ahead to 1976, when the BBC Charter and the life of ITV's regulator were due to expire. The civil service's cautious calculation was that an inquiry might take three years (compared with Pilkington's two), and consequential legislation another two. Moreover, on general constitutional grounds, enquiry by independent committee is necessary in order that the two broadcasting authorities should be accountable, and be seen to be accountable, to the public.

Belatedly, this view prevailed – but too late. The day after Annan's inquiry was announced, parliament was dissolved, Harold Wilson – to most people's surprise – lost the election to Edward Heath, and within a month Annan's appointment was rescinded by the new minister, the former international athlete and ITN newscaster, Christopher Chataway. He made clear that the rebuff to Annan was political, not personal. The Conservative government was reluctant to pull up broadcasting by its roots in order to examine their health, and remained so for the four years of its term.

All that Chataway agreed to was the de-restriction of broadcasting hours, which helped ITV's revenue. This was fiercely resisted by the BBC, for whom extra hours meant extra costs, not income; but Chataway mollified the BBC by continuing to withhold the fourth channel from ITV. He then compensated ITV by easing the burden of the levy on advertising. His successor as minister, Sir John Eden, also resisted persistent lobbying by ITV and its regulator for the creation of ITV2.

Thanks to Heath's handling of the miners' strike, Wilson was returned to power in February 1974. He abolished the ministry of posts and telecommunications he had invented, and handed broadcasting to the Home Office, where Roy Jenkins and his close associate Lord Harris presided. Within weeks, Annan had been re-instated. The four-year gap meant that both the BBC Charter and the life of the ITV system had to be extended to 1979.

The choice of Committee members proved highly contentious. A constant re-balancing of interests saw the numbers swell to sixteen. Even so, the absence of any obvious friend of ITV triggered protests to the government. Annan himself later conceded that "the composition of the Committee was modelled by politics...and for good reason: broadcasting itself has become a political subject".

Perhaps it was therefore fitting that the Annan Report itself eventually became a political victim. It was published in March 1977, a good two years before the next general election was expected, yet a Labour government contrived once again to fail to implement the key proposals of a broadcasting report it had commissioned – indeed, commissioned twice in this case.

The main prize in Annan's gift was the award of the vacant fourth terrestrial television channel. Through its own ineptitude, Labour allowed a Conservative Home Secretary to make the final decision. As a final irony, history repeated itself. In 1954, the Conservative government had disappointed its own hard-working lobbyists by imposing a formidable regulatory structure on the ITV their efforts had brought into existence. In 1980, William Whitelaw abandoned his own party manifesto pledge to allocate the fourth channel to ITV2 and, instead, set Channel 4 on its unique course.

If the creation and implementation of Annan were driven by electoral outcomes, a broader politics shaped the genesis and contents of the Report. However controversial Pilkington's tone and recommendations may have been, the only substantial issue that Committee faced was the merits or demerits of ITV. But broadcasting changed dramatically in the years after Pilkington.

Most obviously, the introduction of BBC2 in 1964 and then colour television in 1967 transformed the BBC, financially, creatively and organisationally. At launch, BBC2 had been funded out of the licence fee, despite the fact that even five years later a quarter of the country could still not receive a signal. This appeared to breach the principle enunciated by Beveridge and Pilkington that the BBC's different UK services should be funded by those who used them.

But in 1968, once BBC2 started colour transmissions, a colour supplement of £5 was added to the underlying £5 fee for a combined radio and television licence. This temporarily restored the theoretical attribution of specific incomes for distinct services. More importantly, it created an engine for the BBC's revenue growth – further fuelled by the conversion of ITV and BBC1 to colour in 1969. In just eight years a majority of television households switched to colour: 9.3 million by 1976, leaving just 8.3 million in black and white. At the same time, staff numbers at the BBC swelled from 17,000 to 26,000, and expenditure from £30m annually at the time of Pilkington to over £200m by the time Annan reported.

Meanwhile, sound-only licences declined in number, to the point where the £1.25 fee became uneconomical to collect in the face of rapidly rising inflation. Annan later pointed out that the 25% of licence fee revenue allocated to radio amounted to much more than would have been provided by the sound-only licence together with the sound element in the combined licence. It would therefore be counter-productive as well as impractical for the sound-only licence to be re-introduced.

The principle of separate funding for separate services was not entirely abandoned. Annan recommended that the BBC give up local radio, on the grounds that the licence fee should not be used for services unobtainable by most licence fee payers. But this proposal was rejected, and what had once been a central tenet of BBC funding faded into history, with no public debate.

Far more a matter of public concern was the BBC's response to the advent of pirate radio in 1964. The Labour government eventually introduced legislation to ban the pirates, but extracted from the BBC in return a commitment to fill the pop music gap so created. This in turn drove the BBC to abandon its careful mix of programmes across its three services and replace it with four generic services, including a pop station.

So William Haley's vision of a pyramid of taste slowly aspiring upwards was finally laid to rest with the publication of *Broadcasting In The Seventies* in 1969. The shock for older BBC listeners was profound. After all, this was an institution which had declined to broadcast pre-race betting odds until 1961, and had banned any reference to royalty, politics, sex or religion in its comedies until 1963. Now, the BBC's expansion, the inflow of young and adventurous producers to BBC2, and the more liberal atmosphere engendered by Director-General Hugh Greene triggered a backlash.

On one side, organisations like the National Viewers and Listeners Association and the Festival of Light protested against the retreat from traditional standards. Conversely, re-structuring of the BBC as a business in the early 1970s, after five years of management consultancy by McKinsey and Company, persuaded the political radicals of the 1960s that the BBC was part of a broadcast system closely held by narrow political, institutional and financial interests.

The cynical transfer in 1967 of ex-Tory minister Lord Hill from the ITA chairmanship to that of the BBC was widely interpreted as a snub inflicted by Harold Wilson on Hugh Greene for the sin of being too independently minded. That Hill was replaced by a former Labour chief whip, Bert Bowden, elevated to the peerage as Lord Aylestone, only confirmed the conspiracy theorists in their worst suspicions. Ironically, Hill's BBC then enraged the outgoing Labour leadership by showing a documentary a year after they lost office entitled *Yesterday's Men*. This further politicised the debate about broadcasting, the authorities that ran it, and its place in a free society. It was within this context that the Annan Committee took shape, and took evidence.

Annan was explicit in acknowledging the nature and intensity of the debate. "Dedicated to the outworn concepts of balance and impartiality, how can the broadcasters reflect the multitude of opinions in our pluralist society?" he asked. The 750 submissions and tens of thousands of letters the committee received – weighing in total some seventeen stone (approx 108 Kilos) – were filled, said Annan with demands that we should re-examine the whole structure of broadcasting and the political assumptions on which the British system rests. Fifteen years ago people would have found this astonishing.

Equally astonishing – just fifteen years after the BBC's triumph in the Pilkington stakes – was the reversal of fortunes in the official verdicts on the national broadcasters. In part, this could be blamed on the presentations made by the BBC and by the IBA – as the ITA had been re-named after it was allocated responsibility for commercial local radio, so now embracing broadcasting rather than just television. The BBC's future Director-General, Ian Trethowan, conceded that the BBC's many submissions were, truth to tell, dull to look at, and dull to read. The ITV companies, by contrast, produced just one report, well-written and most attractively and stylishly presented.

Annan reserved his strongest criticism of the BBC for its current affairs programming. The outcry over *Yesterday's Men* seemed to have blunted the appetite for investigative journalism. "At all levels in the BBC, the row over this unfortunate episode was blamed for the caution, lack of direction, touchiness and unsteadiness in the current affairs output".

There were wider concerns. As the BBC left behind the public service ideals of Reith, Haley and Pilkington, it took on instead an ethos of broadcast professionalism. "The post-1969 reforms," said Annan "moved broadcasting a little further from a 'cultural' activity and a little nearer to a 'business' activity. It was no longer possible to treat broadcasting as setting exemplary standards and providing cultural guidance. The new spirit is now much more managerial. It is concerned with economic management, with the strategy of planning and development, and with maintaining overt control over programmes". How distinctly familiar these observations seem to us today.

If the BBC had sloughed off the occasional arrogance and complacency remarked upon by Beveridge, what replaced them was in Annan's eyes no more attractive. "The BBC today sees itself as beleaguered, pressurised, lobbied and compelled to lobby. The BBC seems to us to have shown some loss of nerve which is partly the cause and partly the result of the barrage of criticism. Its sense of direction has weakened".

Annan was unimpressed by the BBC's contention that its "programmes do not need to be more popular than is necessary to gain and hold 50% of the audience". In his view, "an uninstructed public might be forgiven for believing that the major concern of the BBC's schedulers is to do a piece of no good to ITV". The correct objective, he thought, was not a 50% share, but to "interest and entertain" the audience.

Some of the evidence – and some of the Committee – went well beyond this. The Association of Directors and Producers – a forerunner of the present Directors' Guild – was in sacrificial mood. "We believe, sadly, that the time has now come for this great monolithic sacred cow to be dismembered". Taking their cue, no less than six of the Committee's sixteen members recommended that the BBC be divided into two corporations, television and radio.

They argued that a single corporation, trying to straddle two media, created too large a power bloc and offended against the need for pluralism. They regarded all the friction and complaints as "consequences of the Corporation's unitary control"; conversely, dealing with a myriad of complainants engendered a "permanent defensive posture".

"We consider," said the six, "the position of the Director-General to be an impossible one, paralysed by the over-riding need for consistency, chief executive responsible for assets worth £90m and an income of £200m, editor-in-chief and resident theologian, pope and emperor in one, interpreting and executing one indivisible Corporation".

Even the ten-strong majority conceded that it was a finely balanced argument. Indeed, their reasons for resisting a split were relatively thin – a risk to the BBC's reputation abroad, some loss of influence and independence within the UK, a fear of the government becoming involved in the division of the licence fee revenue, and the prospect of more rather than less bureaucracy. That the dissenting minority was allowed the best tunes was symptomatic of Annan's handling of his large and unwieldy Committee. Throughout the Report are scattered clashing opinions, individual reservations and mutually contradictory positions that are left unresolved.

All this was part of the politicisation of the enquiry process to which Annan himself had alluded. For instance, the driving force behind the minority recommendation to split the BBC was Phillip Whitehead, a noted television producer and Labour MP who, inside and outside Parliament, had lobbied hard for the Annan Committee to be established. After Annan had been stood down in 1970, he offered vocal evidence in the 1972 investigation of ITV by the Commons Select Committee on the Nationalised Industries. This cross-party body proved remarkably united in its critique of ITV, quoted approvingly the most extreme of Pilkington's lofty preferences for the pleasures of the few as more intense than those of the many, and concluded by calling for Annan's re-instatement. Whitehead was quickly on his feet the night the Committee's report was published, calling for "exhaustive analysis" of the "inextricably political and social" issues in broadcasting, which only a committee of inquiry could provide.

Annan had fiercely resisted Whitehead's appointment to his Committee. He wanted no MPs, in line with Pilkington's membership. In fact, the choice of Whitehead seems to have been as a substitute for the preferred representative of the radical groups seeking thorough reform of broadcasting that had sprung up at the end of the 1960s, ranging from the Free Communications Group to the Standing Conference On Broadcasting, or SCOB. The leading light was Anthony Smith, later President of Magdalen College, Oxford, but then a writer and researcher who, as a television producer, had been a contemporary of Whitehead's both at Oxford and in BBC TV current affairs.

It was Smith who dreamed up the big idea that emerged from the hothouse of debate on the left. He proposed that a National Television Foundation be created, to act as a pure publisher, and use the vacant fourth channel to broadcast a wide range of programmes from independent producers and educational and cultural sources. Rumour had it that Smith was personally vetoed by Harold Wilson himself as a member of the Annan Committee.

Whitehead was close to Home Office ministers. His appointment forced Annan to seek balance, in the shape of a Conservative MP (who promptly gave up his seat before the second of 1974's elections), and of another – right of centre – television professional: Antony Jay, the *Yes, Minister* scriptwriter. And if anyone thought the exclusion of Smith had scuppered the National Television Foundation, they had reckoned without Whitehead, who warmly supported it. Indeed, like another member of the Annan Committee, Professor Hilde Himmelweit, he was a member of SCOB, which – despite its modest public support – was accorded two days to give evidence to the Committee. This gave a further boost to the Foundation idea: so much so, that the IBA and ITV hastily spatchcocked a version of it into their revised proposal for an ITV2.

The official history of ITV goes so far as to claim that Whitehead's selection breached normal conventions, which required that appointees to such committees "should, as far as possible, be persons who have not committed themselves so deeply on any side of the questions involved...as to render the probability of an impartial enquiry and a unanimous report practically impossible". This is surely over-dramatic, as is the claim that Whitehead played as significant a role in Annan as Richard Hoggart had played in Pilkington. Annan largely drafted his own Report: what most influenced him was the desire for agreement and the mood of the time.

In at least one respect, ITV's fears proved unfounded. Annan admitted that "we received very little evidence about ITV programmes", and concluded that "ITV has come a long way since the Pilkington Committee reported", and had "improved immensely". In particular, its news and current affairs compared favourably with the BBC's. Even Sir Kenneth Clark, first chairman of the ITA, who had famously rubbished television and the ill effects of competition to Pilkington, was now willing to admit that, thanks to the "spur of competition", television, including ITV, had done a "remarkable" amount of good.

By this time, of course, Clark had delivered a landmark documentary series to the BBC which had earned him the soubriquet of Lord Clark of Civilization. Without a hint of irony, Annan quoted Clark approvingly – "far from having debased public taste, he thought it had always been a little ahead of it. It had enormously widened people's horizons". He then went out of his way to reject what he called "the most controversial proposal of the Pilkington Committee", recommendation 43, which sought to transfer the functions of scheduling and airtime sales from the ITV companies to their regulator.

The reasons given for such rejection do not bear close scrutiny: it would appear that Annan was simply balancing his ticket, for, despite the severity of his criticisms of the BBC, his final verdict was that the BBC still gave "a better all-round service to the public than ITV", which, for all its progress, "could do better yet".

Perhaps this was just a post hoc rationalisation to explain Annan's most important decision – to deny a second channel to ITV. What drove this decision – a unanimous one – was the zeitgeist: the widely-held belief that to leave control of television within the hands of the BBC/IBA duopoly would be a profound error. Annan consciously adopted the adjective coined by Anthony Smith: the strait-jacket.

Smith told Annan that the creation of ITV2 would "complete the symmetrical strait-jacket of broadcasting in Britain and continue it for ever. Awarding a new channel or even a substantial part of it to the IBA and the companies would damage broadcasting irreparably. Better no to award it at all than to place it in these particular wrong hands".

Annan reproduced this verbatim. In defining his key three tasks, he identified preserving accountability through Parliament and the editorial independence of the broadcasters. But above all he wanted diversity, which "cannot be achieved in the future if all developments are forced into the strait-jacket of the existing duopoly of the BBC and IBA".

If, for Reith, the whole point of broadcasting had been unitary control, for Annan the key word was diversity. And in adopting such a stance, he also rejected the Reithian view of the power of broadcasting. Although a majority of the Committee paid lip service to Pilkington's formula that, until there was proof to the contrary, the effect of television must be assumed to be direct, like water dripping on a stone, Annan's own view – which he confusingly ascribed to the "great majority" of his Committee – was this: "television may influence us directly or indirectly in the goods we buy, but, except for those people who are emotionally disturbed...it is unlikely to cause us to commit violent crimes or change our deeply held moral or political beliefs".

The logic of such a position forced Annan to reject as "deceptively simple" the old argument for broadcasting to provide moral uplift. "Too often those who advocate such a policy seem to suppose that social and moral objectives could be formulated, agreed, and then imposed on the broadcasters. No doubt they can in totalitarian countries. They cannot here. We do not accept that it is part of the broadcasters' function to act as arbiters of morals or manners, or set themselves up as social engineers".

Instead, Annan retreated to broadcasting as being nothing more than the sum of the programmes being broadcast. Having rejected moral uplift, he saw virtue in the argument for breaking up the old power structure and creating more diversity. He was, of course, still a social engineer; but in the tinkering, rather than the towering, business. What he sought was "adjustments in the relationship between the broadcasters, the Government and the public".

Instinctively, he shied away from proposals from the left for an over-arching Communications Council – as advocated by the Labour Party – or a Broadcasting Commission, such as that supported by SCOB. He saw in these a "return to the monolithic control of broadcasting, which we have not had for 21 years". As a consequence, there would be "rigidity, limitation of choice, a threat to freedom of expression and of political interference, and spreading bureaucratisation". The Committee was therefore "unanimous in believing that an executive Broadcasting Commission would be insufferable. However pure and valiant [it] might be in its early days, it would in the end become...a self-serving and self-perpetuating power group".

To all this, Annan preferred diversity, even at the expense of less efficient use of resources. Likening the contest between the BBC and the IBA to that between the Montagues and the Capulets, he came to a sweeping conclusion: "we believe the duopoly should come to an end during the period we are reviewing". By this he meant the next twelve to fifteen years, and what he proposed was a general re-structuring of the broadcasting institutions, re-shaping the IBA and the BBC, and inventing two new authorities. Annan later revealed that the entire scheme, including the division of the BBC, had sprung fully-formed from the mouth of Phillip Whitehead in ten short minutes at a Committee away-day. Annan adopted it almost wholesale, shorn only of the BBC split.

He wanted local radio taken away from the IBA and the BBC, to be run by a Local Radio Authority. Concluding that "local radio is in a mess", he observed that "as long as local radio is an appendage of the BBC or the IBA it cannot hope to be the first priority". As a consequence, the ITA would be re-named the Regional Television Authority, to reflect the federal structure of the system it regulated. To complete the picture, an Open Broadcasting Authority would be created to run the fourth channel – "a publisher of programme material supplied by others".

That this was merely another name for the National Television Foundation the Committee made no effort to disguise. "By far the most comprehensive scheme came from Mr Anthony Smith, who proposed that such was the flourishing state of broadcasting in this country that the time had come when a National Television Foundation should be set up". In Smith's words, it would have "a kind of impresario role, merely allocating resources to some but fitting producers, writers, technicians to others who arrive only with an idea, a grievance or a cause".

This vision suited Annan's purposes well. "We are convinced that this is the right approach to the fourth channel. A great opportunity would be missed if the fourth channel were seen solely in terms of extending the *present* range of programmes," which would be a recipe for "a self-destructive battle for ratings". What the Committee saw in the OBA was not only "an addition to the plurality of outlets, but a force for plurality in a deeper sense... It should be a test-bed for experiment and symbolize all the vitality, new initiatives, practices and liberties which could inspire broadcasters".

In rejecting ITV2, Annan could not resist a sideswipe at the BBC. In an amusing re-run of the arguments to Pilkington concerning the third channel, when the ITA had disingenuously proposed an education channel in order to head off (unsuccessfully) BBC2, so Annan dismissed the BBC's proposal for a specialist audiences network. "The IBA," he said "regarded the BBC's comments as gratuitous: their sole intention was to do ITV a bit of no good" – a distinctly Annanite expression we have heard before – "and prevent the fourth channel going their way".

The OBA squared the broadcasting circle for Annan. He was nervous of the call for greater accountability to the public by the broadcasters. He also rejected the idea of a general right of access to the media. In broad terms, he was content with the "chain of accountability" as he called it, which was from broadcast authorities to Parliament, and from broadcasters to broadcast authorities. Parliament should decide the number and nature of broadcast services, but thereafter not intervene. Broadcast authorities should "take broadcasters by the elbow rather than twist their arm" – "censure not censor". Now the OBA would offer an even looser rein, as a publisher more than a regulator.

Unfortunately, this neat solution ran into a practical problem. Annan had already adopted another liberal pseudo-principle, often advanced by broadcast theorists as one of the strengths of the British system in the way it seemed to deflect direct competition for audiences. "As far as possible, each Broadcasting Authority should have its own source or sources of revenue and should not have to compete with other Broadcasting Authorities for the same source of revenue".

In truth, such a principle could only be stated ex post facto rather than a priori: and the OBA simply did not fit the useful but accidental pattern of the past. Anthony Smith had imagined a control mechanism with "virtually no employees", and with programmes financed by an annual fixed sum from advertising, from sponsorship and from payments by education authorities. It was by no means clear how sufficient money could be raised from such sources. Indeed, at one point the Report proposed, in the absence of other revenue, "a Government grant to sustain the novelty of the channel and its productions, either directly or possibly through the Arts Council". Annan himself subsequently conceded that "how the channel was to be financed was a matter on which we disagreed".

This insouciance struck the IBA as simply perverse. Its Director-General condemned Annan's proposals as illogical, naïve, ill-thought-out and unrealistic. The verdict in the official history of ITV is scathing: "to all except the small lobby which had promoted it with such fervour, [the OBA] appeared patently impractical and a dead duck politically before the ink was dry on the report".

Disappointment amongst those furthest left was even more outspoken. "In line with Annan's general thinking," wrote Professor Nicholas Garnham, "the OBA is going to encourage diversity, pluralism and creative freedom by being structure-less. This improbable feat is achieved precisely, as its critics have rightly and with some well-directed ribaldry pointed out, by giving the new Authority no conceivably realistic source of funds".

Garnham's attack went far beyond the inadequacies of the OBA: "what the Annan Committee has done is, paradoxically, to discredit structural change by partially endorsing it. Many, both inside and outside broadcasting, put much faith in the radical possibilities of a Committee of Inquiry and actively campaigned, against Government opposition and inertia, for such a committee to be set up. As the post-Annan debate...has shown more clearly than the report itself, the mood has decisively changed to one of a weary and fatalistic acceptance of the status quo. Indeed it is possible to sustain the cynical argument that Annan, like all such Committees of Inquiry, was expressly designed to lance the boil of radical discontent".

Of course, that is a verdict after the event, and it was surely beyond even such a brilliant mind as Annan's to appease the left with a radical version of the fourth channel, but cunningly leave it without resources. The fault was in the original design. Although Anthony Smith dismissed criticisms of the Foundation from the left as reflecting unrealistic aspirations for wholesale change – which he dubbed "Garnham-vision" – the weakness of the OBA lay in its financing.

Surprisingly, the OBA – at least in name – survived the next stage of governmental action, in the shape of a White Paper that emerged a year after Annan published his Report. This outcome, however, was already heavily compromised. The Home Office, supported by the Treasury, had tried to drop the OBA in favour of ITV2. But a leak of the proposal to Phillip Whitehead allowed a rearguard action time to deflect this. The OBA survived – just – but within a framework of broadcasting measures that included the creation of three BBC management boards, half of whose members would be appointed by the Government. So unappealing was this latest document that few mourned its demise, along with the Callaghan administration, in the 1979 general election.

To general astonishment, the new Home Office team of William Whitelaw and Leon Brittan seemed disinclined to enact their own manifesto commitment to ITV2. Instead, they embarked on a careful tour of the options. The reformists revived their campaign in the shape of the Channel Four Group, whose organiser was a recent media studies graduate called Michael Jackson. Under pressure from Whitelaw, the IBA repeatedly modified its proposals, until the ITV element had been reduced to proportions that the insurgents – and Whitelaw – found acceptable.

In a moment of hubris, Annan claimed the credit. "The OBA," he told the House of Lords, "was born from an idea of Mr Tony Smith...our Committee took that piece of dough and began to bake it. I do not think we got very far in the baking before we had to finish our report. The new fourth channel is really the same loaf, only now done to a turn". Few would dispute the implication that Annan's OBA was half-baked: remarkably, however, his Report did indeed contain a plan for the precise structure of the future Channel 4, tucked away in Chapter 15, paragraph 7.

The Association of Directors and Producers had a novel proposal. They suggested that the fourth channel should be allocated to the programme makers. The IBA should schedule the channel as a complementary offering to ITV1. Certainly the ITV companies would contribute but so would independent production companies, whose work should be fostered, and where necessary, financed by the channel. The channel would not need production facilities or studios apart from those necessary for presentation and continuity: all it required was a small staff with a chief executive and executive board and a secretariat under the overall aegis of the IBA. They would purchase and process productions. The IBA would finance the channel by imposing a levy on the ITV companies, who would have the exclusive right to sell advertising time on the new channel in their own areas. The channel itself would be a non-profit-making organisation.

The unofficial historian of Channel 4 has warned against seeing a direct route between this proposal and the eventual outcome, regretting its "address to expediency" as compared with the idealism of the National Television Foundation. As it happens, the ADP document, far from being novel, was a re-draft of a proposal formulated by John Birt and myself in 1973, and endorsed by Jeremy Isaacs, who subsequently became Channel 4's first Chief Executive. Its first priority was a funding mechanism that worked, around which could be built a structure which encouraged pluralism and diversity. The authors consciously looked back to Pilkington's famous recommendation 43, separating the process of commissioning and scheduling programmes from that of selling advertising.

Whitelaw's eventual endorsement of the mechanism and structure was all the more creditable for the politically sensitive aspect that Annan had correctly identified – the inevitable call on public money. Such a Channel 4 might not be a direct charge on the public purse, but insofar as its funding would be a first call on the levy payments by the ITV companies, there would inevitably be a reduction in Treasury receipts for some years, at least until the total audience for ITV and Channel 4 earned sufficient extra revenue to offset the additional cost of Channel 4's programmes.

The Welsh Fourth Channel – a last-minute fudge by Whitelaw under pressure from a Welsh nationalist MP threatening to fast until death – proved an even bigger drain on the Treasury: but a boon for the aerial industry, which sold special equipment to tens of thousands of non-Welsh speaking homes in Wales keen to see the English version of Channel 4.

As it has turned out, under Jeremy Isaacs' leadership, Channel 4 delivered much of what Anthony Smith's Foundation had envisaged. Seen by many as the intellectual father of the channel, Smith was duly offered a seat on the channel's board, graciously acknowledging that the ADP funding structure ignored for so long had proved to be the best way forward.

Annan was less gracious, continuing to claim many years later that Channel 4 was set up on the lines he had suggested, despite the utterly different structure of the OBA concept. No wonder Annan disparaged the ADP proposal as "novel" and thereafter ignored it. He understood it neither then, nor a decade later.

Channel 4 marked the high point of social engineering in British broadcasting. It carefully placed the new channel in the context of the existing channels, and minimised its competitive impact on the system. In Annan's slightly crude formulation, "there are enough programmes for the majority – what is needed now is programmes for the different minorities which add up to make the majority". Whitelaw's Channel 4 improbably delivered much of what Annan had imagined but which his Report had signally failed to make real.

In many other respects, the Report proved to be equally unproductive. The IBA was left untouched – only much later was commercial radio detached from it, and even then the BBC was left with its own local radio network. The proposed exclusion of advertisements from children's programmes was rejected, as was the proposed ban on dubbed laughter.

Having themselves rejected a permanent Broadcasting Commission, and even Anthony Smith's proposed National Broadcasting Centre as "at best a perpetual fidget and at worst an incubus hovering over all aspects of broadcasting", the Annan Committee had come up with a Public Enquiry Board for Broadcasting, which would hold major hearings every seven years – a kind of intermittent Annan, which would, for instance, advise on the allocation of the fifth channel. This, too, failed to find favour. The only modest structural change Annan accomplished was the creation of a Broadcasting Complaints Commission to deal with allegations of unfair treatment of individuals and invasions of privacy.

How well spent was the Annan Committee's £315,000 cost? It is much admired as a statement of liberal principles at a politically turbulent time. It managed to straddle many conflicting views. Perhaps as a result, it has proved a poor guide to the future. It imagined that by 1991 the most likely technical advance in broadcasting would be the public use of teletext. Like the BBC and the IBA, it doubted whether video-recorders would have mass sales, being seen as primarily of educational use and otherwise only of appeal to "the minority that is acutely choosy". Annan even feared that the attraction of VCRs to wealthy minorities might lead to certain types of programming disappearing from broadcast television onto VCR distribution.

With a touch more realism, Annan predicted that "the biggest threat to the present concept of the mass audience watching a programme financed exclusively by one broadcasting organisation is undoubtedly cable". But at that point the Committee's vision failed them. "We do not see cable in the next fifteen years developing as a national service. We consider it will develop as a local community service. We do not see cable services being developed as Pay Television".

As for satellite television, all that was in prospect was a five-channel service delivered by prohibitively-expensive high-powered transmission. Annan instinctively allocated this to the BBC, which – to the Corporation's delight – he designated as "the instrument of national broadcasting". Even the fourth channel was seen by Annan as a remote prospect "in the present economic climate", as he put it. And despite reminding the pessimists of their false prediction that there would be "insufficient professional talent" to service BBC2, he declared that "the prospect that a fifth channel could provide much the same fare at the same level of excellence [as existing channels] seems dubious". On that point, at least, the jury is still out.

At the end of 174 recommendations, few of which were to have any impact, Annan offered his final hostage to fortune. "We do not foresee in the fifteen years ahead the possibility of financing any major technological development such as will change the face of broadcasting". He had particular doubts about cable. Yet within five years, the new government, marching to a very different drum, had launched an urgent inquiry into the prospects for cable television. The shift from the classical liberalism of Annan to the market philosophies of the 1980s is the subject of the next two lectures.

[4]
Hunt

4 March 1999

In 1924, in Hythe, near Southampton, Mr A W Morton connected his radio set by wire to a loudspeaker in another room in his house, so that his wife could listen there. A year later, he had extended the wire to 25 of his neighbours, charging them 7p a week – one shilling and sixpence in pre-decimal money. So was born the cable distribution system in this country.

By the 1980s, it had enlarged on a commercial basis to serve 14 percent of all UK homes; but it was an essentially passive system, apart from occasional experiments in community programming, pay-per-view and film subscription. Attempts to expand beyond merely relaying the existing terrestrial channels had always been thwarted. In 1982, official policy underwent a sea change. Politicians saw cable as a new Klondyke. And the instrument of change was a report written by a three-man committee of inquiry chaired by Lord Hunt.

Of all the reports I will be considering in this series of lectures, that by Lord Hunt is probably the least well known. Indeed, some people might well ask how so slim a volume – just 46 pages, produced at a cost of a mere £45,000 – can claim to be considered alongside the big beasts of Beveridge, Pilkington and Annan, let alone the subsequent Peacock. But the Hunt Report marks an extraordinary shift in the entire approach to broadcasting in the UK, all the more remarkable because it followed so swiftly from the apogee of the previous consensus – the creation of Channel 4 as a deliberate extension of the public service principle which had prevailed for sixty years.

Even more curious is that this very Channel 4 – a prime example of social engineering – had been steered onto the statute book by the Home Secretary in the new Thatcher administration, rescuing it from the half-thought-through meanderings of the Annan Committee appointed – twice! – by Labour. Willie Whitelaw delivered a new channel that drained money from the Treasury, served minorities rather than commerce, and left the old ITV monopoly of advertising time untouched – about as un-Thatcherite an outcome as could have been imagined. But within months of the passage of the 1980 Broadcasting Act, the Home Office found itself under increasing pressure from the Cabinet Office and Department of Industry to address the alluring prospects of cable and satellite television.

As far as satellite was concerned, Whitelaw took his cue from Annan. A new international agreement in 1977 had created the opportunity for each European country to launch a high-powered satellite capable of delivering some five new services to small dishes attached to residences – a system described as direct broadcasting by satellite, or DBS. Annan had recommended allocating all these channels to the BBC. Whitelaw, more cautiously, invited the BBC to take up the first two, and held the other three in reserve.

No sooner had the Home Office published its plans for DBS in 1981 than an Information Technology Advisory Panel was created within the Cabinet Office to pursue the possibility of encouraging a moribund cable industry to offer pay television services. It may surprise us today to learn that in 1981 there were 2.6 million homes connected to cable systems. Nearly half of these were blocks of flats served by a single roof-top antenna that spread the various channels by wire to all residents. The remainder were served by limited-capacity cable systems installed to overcome the inadequacies of VHF transmission before UHF broadcasting was introduced. A typical charge for such a commercial service was £15 per annum.

In practice, all that these services offered was simply a relay of the terrestrial channels. Hopes of turning them into proper subscription services had long met strong opposition. Pilkington had objected in principle to pay television, on the grounds that it might divert programming away from free television. Worse, it would fail to meet the purposes of broadcasting, as perceived by Pilkington, in that it would inevitably pursue majority audiences. "No service of subscription television [should] be authorised", he concluded.

Annan was utterly dismissive of subscription funding. He saw the future of cable in local television, not pay television. "As the BBC and IBA extend the coverage of their UHF transmitters, there are going to be fewer and fewer people willing to pay a cable company to provide what they can get off-air...we were not persuaded that Pay TV of itself generated new programme material...it was therefore a ravenous parasite. Moreover, if Pay TV were commercially successful, there could well be less choice in the long run for most viewers. Pay TV organisations would probably be able to afford to buy exclusive rights in some events which are now broadcast generally by the BBC or the IBA".

Annan was not persuaded that protecting named events would be enough. "Nevertheless there would be a real danger that the range of programming available to the public from the broadcasting organisations would be reduced. Certainly it would reduce the possibilities of programming on the fourth channel. None of us, therefore, considers that a service of Pay TV based primarily on feature films and live coverage of sporting events can be regarded as a high priority and most of us recommend that the cable operators should not be authorised to provide Pay TV services".

Indeed, Annan was hostile to any significant expansion of television: "better to have fewer services adequately financed than more of abysmal quality" – a forerunner of the "more means worse" school of thinking that would rapidly grow in the 1980s.

Despite this fierce onslaught, the Labour government, in its White Paper responding to Annan, chose to authorise a handful of pay television cable trials – thirteen in all, serving a few hundred thousand homes. But Labour shared Annan's instinct that any large-scale development of cable should be centrally funded. Thatcher's ministers sustained the trials, but had no interest in a publicly-funded cable system. Yet they were deeply attracted by the industrial and commercial prospects offered by cable: information technology was starting to take hold, and the job and export opportunities seemed limitless.

Kenneth Baker, who had been given the title of Minister for Industry and Information Technology, was quite explicit in a Commons debate: "the reason we want to move quickly is [that] with cabling more jobs will be created". Although entertainment would be the driver, "the range of non-broadcasting services is the raison d'être of the expansion". Cultural issues were being displaced by industrial priorities.

As a result, throughout the decade, a recurring theme would be the competition between the Home Office and industry ministers for control of the broadcasting agenda. Mrs Thatcher had already decided on the privatisation and de-regulation of British Telecom, and had encouraged the emergence of a competitor in the shape of Mercury. She noted the French government's encouragement of cable and subscription television, and was persuaded that a new industrial revolution could be built on the back of the wiring of Britain. What that wiring needed was the engine of entertainment to drive it along, whatever that meant in terms of the concept and practice of public service broadcasting.

Towards the end of the 1980s, the Department of Trade and Industry, supported by the Treasury, attempted taking primary control of broadcasting. Special advisers – typically, Thatcher's favourite industrialists – would organise breakfasts to decide the future of television without a Home Office minister in sight. Broadcasting legislation was decided by a cabinet committee which excluded the broadcasting minister.

On one spectacular occasion, the Trade and Industry Secretary, Lord Young, announced that BBC2 and Channel 4 would be shifted to direct broadcast by satellite, releasing their terrestrial frequencies to the commercial market: a proposal *The Guardian* characterised as "simultaneously lunatic and sinister". It was swiftly withdrawn, to barely concealed glee from Home Office officials: but that such a proposal could be made without their knowledge simply illustrated how impatient Mrs Thatcher had become with those she considered to be blocking the path to industrial prosperity.

At the beginning of the decade, she looked to ad hoc groups such as the Information Technology Advisory Panel, made up essentially of electronics industry executives, "to ensure that government policies and actions are securely based on a close appreciation of market needs and opportunities". The ITAP report on cable was published in March 1982. It wanted restrictions on cable programming removed, authorisation of local networks of 30 or more channels, and a rapid declaration by the government of its policy intentions. "Only through a set of speedy, positive and radical regulatory changes can the United Kingdom obtain the benefits offered by developments in cable technology... for British industry, a late decision is the same as a negative decision".

Curiously, one of the reasons for ITAP's pressure was a fear that satellite development might have moved too far ahead if cable was not quickly de-regulated – and it was cable, with its return path capability and potential for interactivity and transactions, which was seen as the main source of subsequent industrial benefit. An early expansion of cable would then make it the natural distribution medium for DBS entertainment services. The ITAP Report believed original expectations that satellite receiver and decoder boxes would cost only £150 were too optimistic – perhaps £400 would be nearer the mark, making a cable build-out even more imperative. The ITAP calculation was that to cable 50% of Britain would cost £2.5 billion, but that the eventual benefits for the country would be more than a billion pounds annually.

Immediately, the Home Office tried to re-capture the initiative by appointing a three-man team that same month to take up the ITAP challenge and recommend on the future of cable. The Committee was chaired by Lord Hunt, who, as Sir John Hunt, had been Cabinet Secretary up till 1979. He was joined by Sir Maurice Hodgson, a former chairman of ICI, and the physicist Professor James Ring, who had been for many years a member of ITV's regulatory body, the IBA. A notable omission was that of an economist, which left the Committee's findings open to heavy criticism from free-marketeers once they were published.

Hunt's frame of reference was narrowly defined: its remit was "the government's wish to secure the benefits for the United Kingdom which cable technology can offer and its willingness to consider the expansion of cable systems which would permit cable to carry a wider range of entertainment and other services (including when available direct broadcasting by satellite), but in a way consistent with the wider public interest, in particular the safeguarding of public service broadcasting". He was given just six months to complete his report.

Critics from the left seized on this tight brief as evidence that the decision had already been taken. The Campaign for Press and Broadcasting Freedom bitterly complained that Hunt had been given no room for manoeuvre by such a clearly-stated set of government preferences, let alone enough time to read the 189 submissions. Hunt demurred: he claimed six months to have been sufficient and that his Committee was at liberty to reject the expansion of cable if it could not be squared with the interests of public service broadcasting. His solution was to position cable as supplementary to the terrestrial broadcasters, widening consumer choice by providing local, niche, specialist and minority channels. Hunt did not believe that "channels of general entertainment in direct competition with those of the BBC and ITV" would be created by cable.

Hunt reminded his readers that the seemingly large base of cabled homes was a mirage. "There are no modern cable systems in this country," he said. "We have some ageing narrowband systems, which do no more than relay public service broadcasts except in the case of a handful of pilot schemes of subscription television and a single channel consisting almost entirely of films".

He shared the view that the replacement of these systems with modern wideband cable would not be possible without entertainment-driven investment. He acknowledged that there were fears of an expansion of television leading to a decline in standards, and also of the best (or most popular) programming migrating from free-to-air television to subscription channels if they became widespread. Nonetheless, he felt a balance could be struck.

"We believe that recent developments both in multi-channel cable technology and indeed in public service broadcasting itself justify a reassessment of the arguments against subscription television which the Pilkington and Annan reports found convincing. We are however satisfied that some limited safeguards against damage to public service broadcasting will be necessary in the interest of the large sections of the community who, through choice or necessity, will remain dependent on it".

Hunt confessed that "cable television is in many ways a leap into the dark". He saw it as "all about widening the viewer's choice" rather than becoming "another branch of public service broadcasting". In his view, "the whole approach needs to be different" to reflect the multiplicity of narrowcast services that cable would be able to offer. As new channels would be of "special interest" or "locally orientated", he saw no need for broadcast-style regulation. Rather, he imagined an "oversight" function, with "a few general guidelines", direct regulation only becoming necessary if self-regulation failed.

He shied away from the bold vision of electronic publishing that Peter Jay had set out in his influential Mactaggart Lecture at the 1981 Edinburgh International Television Festival. Hunt did not see cable as ready for the role of publisher, subject only to the law of the land. His arguments against Jayvision, as it became called, were pragmatic rather than logical – cable was not fully spread, there was not enough capacity, and the power of the image was stronger than that of the written word. It was Peacock who would be more persuaded by Jay.

In structural terms, Hunt was willing to allow a large degree of vertical integration between those who laid the cable, those who managed it, those who supplied channels to it, and those who supplied programming to the channels. The Committee members noted warnings from the US as to the dangers of "ownership links between cable operators and programme providers", but "we do not think there will be real risks from such vertical integration in the country in the foreseeable future: indeed, the problem is more likely to be one of a shortage of good material rather than good material not finding an outlet".

Hunt fully realised that the government had no intention of paying for the cabling of Britain, despite the ambitions in this direction within the Labour Party and interested parties like the Post Office Engineering Union. In such circumstances, there could be no question of regarding cable as a common carrier of all signals seeking carriage, even if there were no capacity constraints. Instead, the old requirement for a Wireless Telegraphy licence would be dropped in favour of a simple local franchising process, whereby effective local monopolies would be granted in exchange for commitments to build the system. Local authorities hostile to cable or this franchising process would not be permitted to frustrate an operator by withholding permission to take up paving stones.

Hunt saw no need for particular ownership restrictions, except where political and religious groups were concerned, though he did seek to exclude foreigners – which at that point included Europeans – from majority control of any franchise. Nor was multiple franchise ownership an issue – "we see little danger of a monopoly arising from excessive ownership of cable franchises".

Programmes transmitted right across the cable network would be welcome: "Cable operators in our view should have freedom to provide programmes which are likely to appeal to their customers, even though some of these may be provided by national programme providers to a large number of cable operators".

Curiously, though, Hunt was bearish about the prospects for subscription. Apart from films and the BBC's DBS offerings, he was "satisfied that the number of additional channels for which most people are prepared to pay extra is limited". The Committee contented itself by recommending that "subscription for particular channels should be allowed". Hunt was unconvinced by cable's experience in America, believing, a little quaintly, that its rise had been caused, not by the inherent attractiveness of pay television, the weakness of terrestrial signals or the meagre nature of public television, but by the "intrusiveness of broadcast television advertising".

In the UK, he said, "for most people the presence of advertising does not affect the decision whether or not to watch a particular programme. Thus the motivation to pay for subscription television may be weaker here than in the United States, and as a consequence subscriptions may be a less buoyant source of finance". By this convoluted logic, he then concluded that cable would need advertising revenue, and that there should be no limit on advertising breaks – flying in the face of his observations of the American scene.

An equally odd line of logic led Hunt to ban pay-per-view as a method of funding. "The BBC represented very strongly that one of their main concerns about cable competition lay in the possible siphoning of sporting events from free television. We have concluded that it would be safer for the time being to preclude pay-per-view programmes being offered on cable systems". He frankly admitted that this did not prevent "siphoning to subscription services – but it does at least avoid the problem in its most acute form". After all, he argued, pay-per-view was not that important for cable, but a ban would provide "a measure of reassurance for public service broadcasting".

The most sensitive target of potential siphoning by cable was the list of national sporting events to which broadcasters were forbidden from acquiring exclusive rights. This item of policy had its origins in the limited geographical coverage of the early ITV stations, which led the BBC to argue – with support from the House of Lords – that it would be wrong to deprive large numbers of viewers out of reach of ITV transmitters of major sports occasions. This had become enshrined in the Broadcasting Act of 1981 as a reserve power of the Home Secretary to bar exclusive contracts with regard to seven listed events, but had never been utilised, thanks to informal non-compete agreements between ITV and the BBC.

Hunt conceded the main point to the terrestrial channels: "The present list of protected events...should apply to new cable services as it applies to broadcasters; apart from this [and pay-per-view generally] we do not think it appropriate to place restrictions on the sporting or other events which cable television may wish to cover" – even "if it could force up the fee for events which are already televised".

In fact, the BBC had a shopping list of protected species that went far beyond the seven major events. It wanted to include rugby union, Open golf, boxing title fights, all the racing classics and the motoring Grand Prix; a further five categories of events shared with ITV, such as European athletics and soccer; ten other named sports and – most interesting of all – "foreign-produced material" as it was called, by which it meant such series as *Kojak*, *Starsky and Hutch*, and *Dallas*.

If cable were allowed to bid for these, said the BBC, we would see either "the majority of viewers deprived of star attractions" or, in fighting off cable's bids, the diversion of BBC resources to the point of "impoverishing creative areas of minority programming".

The logic of the BBC's position was clear. It should be allowed to continue buying existing material as cheaply as in the past. Moreover, the cable companies should be compelled to carry a substantial proportion of originated UK product on all their services, and should be prevented from running American product in substantial volume.

The BBC said to Hunt that

> the introduction of foreign programmes, particularly American, comprising largely trivial entertainment material is in the long term bound to have an effect on viewing habits. Over a period, market forces of this kind could reduce finance available for UK television production. Expressed in extreme terms [and the BBC showed no reluctance so to do] there is a danger that the UK Television Industry could go the same way as the UK Film Industry. This clearly needs to be guarded against, particularly since UK Television is a major force in establishing and maintaining UK identity and its specific cultural value.

Surely, said the BBC, there was enough prospective increase in viewer choice without allowing a free-for-all in cable. "With the arrival of Channel Four, Breakfast Television and DBS, the industry is already being given an opportunity for proper expansion" – as opposed, presumably, to improper expansion – [so] "the BBC calls for regulation to protect the interests of the British viewer and the British Television Industry".

Cable companies should simply provide "local access, ethnic and specialist programmes" – rather like the BBC's view of Channel 4 to Annan. "If they compete with the networks for popular programming, there could be just more of the same" – perish the thought. In its most apocalyptic mode, the BBC warned against "an operating philosophy made up of quick-kill methods of financial control, a cynical view of public taste and no concern for social side-effects".

But Hunt was opposed to specific programming requirements, and made "no recommendation on the range and balance of programmes". There were to be no quotas: film channels were likely to have predominantly American content, and foreign channels, such as RTE, would be welcome additions to the cable scene. For cable to spread rapidly, it needed attractive, low-cost programming requiring a low basic monthly charge – Hunt looked to free-to-air services, the BBC's DBS channels and foreign stations to help drive take-up.

As a modest further reassurance to the terrestrial broadcasters, he ruled that broadband systems must carry "all free broadcast television services serving their particular locality whether present or future", which included at least one of the prospective BBC DBS channels. As a concession to cable, he removed the "must carry" rule for old systems limited to four channels, though only for five years. Then, tacking back in the other direction, he sought to impose the old radio relay rules on cable systems offering radio services. "If channel capacity is no problem, it is only after distributing all the BBC's national services and both local radio services, if there are two serving that area, that a cable operator can choose to relay any other authorised broadcasting station, such as Radio Luxembourg".

So we find the supposed apostle of de-regulation quoting directly from the Pilkington bible. It was no surprise when Welsh cable companies were later forced to carry the new Welsh Fourth Channel in preference to Channel 4 in English, however large a proportion of their customers opposed such an imposition. Yet elsewhere Hunt argued for the right of Welshmen and Scotsmen living in London to receive S4C or STV, even if the universal availability on cable of all ITV stations out of area might eventually undermine the economics of some of them, or even be in breach of transmission rights in acquired programmes.

This haphazard approach to issues irritated the purists. Two free-market economists, Veljanovski and Bishop, in a paper published by the Institute of Economic Affairs, complained of shallowness and incoherence and "a weakness which infects the whole Report: its failure to evince an understanding of the market system in general and the cable industry in particular...as a result, it proceeds from recommendation to recommendation by the force of assertion rather than reasoned argument".

Even so, Hunt's conclusion that cable should be allowed broad freedom to expand must have gladdened the hearts of the cable lobby. Indeed, the Campaign for Press and Broadcasting Freedom complained that the Cable Television Association's evidence had been "taken on board virtually wholesale". Hunt offered minimum constraints, in his own phrase, other than that programming should follow the usual broadcast rules on taste and decency – the only exception being subscription channels with an electronic lock, which would be allowed to show at any time any films certified by the British Board of Film Classification below the adult R18 level.

Hunt also recommended that the only restriction on cable ownership should be a ban on control of any system resting in the hands of a foreign company. He wanted the franchising authority to be a new body, the Cable Television Authority. He feared that putting the IBA in charge might deter investors familiar with its role as a public service broadcasting regulator. This triggered a fierce attack on the Report by the IBA once it was published.

The IBA "totally dissents from the Hunt Inquiry's central belief – that, if its recommendations were accepted, there would be no serious damage to public service broadcasting: the regulatory body proposed by the Inquiry…is to…be ineffective and toothless in the interests of encouraging investment". The IBA had no wish to take on such a feeble role, and predicted that rivalry between regulated and de-regulated broadcasting would be "inevitable and destructive" – which prompted Professor Ring, the Committee member who had served on the IBA, to comment that Hunt had been right not to hand cable to the IBA!

Interestingly, the IBA had been one of the few organisations to have argued in its evidence that subscription would be the primary funder of cable's expansion – a prediction that proved more accurate than Hunt's own.

Hunt's critics were quick to assemble. The ACTT, the television technicians union, described his Report as "a get-rich-quick recipe for the cable buccaneers". The Post Office engineers sneered that "an inferior, outdated, half-baked cable system will appear in some towns and cities". The Labour Party's Roy Hattersley called for "a national network of cable, laid and managed by the government".

Some of the criticisms from the left were themselves contradictory. On the one hand, it was predicted that no new cable would be built – the operators would take advantage of the five-year dispensation from the "must carry" rule for four-channel systems, and substitute pay channels for the free-to-air channels in the areas they already controlled. Alternatively, if that temptation was resisted, the Campaign for Press and Broadcasting Freedom argued that there was "a very real danger that unlimited cable advertising could lead to a desperate scramble for revenue that would be disastrous for commercial television, radio and newspapers".

This theme was taken up by the then Director of Programmes at London Weekend Television. If the Hunt Report were implemented, warned John Birt, "choice will diminish remarkably; and the public service system of broadcasting will quickly decline: this process will occur because of the impoverishing impact Lord Hunt's prescription for cable expansion will have on the finances of ITV and the BBC". Birt believed that "few viewers will find much in this milk-and-water cable service to stimulate, to enthral or to satisfy them"; but even channels with few viewers, if there were enough of them, would collectively lead to ITV's revenue declining in real terms within five years. Quite how this would negatively affect the BBC was not explained, but Birt's solution was for one, and one only, of each type of niche service to be licensed at a time – youth, ethnic, cultural, sport, news. And the whole system needed tight regulation.

The BBC's response was confused: and no doubt heavily influenced by its commitment to DBS – direct broadcasting by satellite. The day before Hunt reported, the BBC had held a press briefing at which, according to one trade paper, it had warned that "the end of broadcasting as we know it was nigh if entertainment-based cable was introduced". The BBC spokesman talked of wall-to-wall *Dallas*: a remarkably derogatory concept coming from the broadcaster that had shamelessly hyped *Dallas* in its own schedule – even on the news – when competing with ITV. Apparently, carefully controlled doses of *Dallas* from the BBC were fine: it was when the patient gained access to unlimited amounts of the substance that "public taste was coarsened", in the BBC's own phrase. But then, this was the BBC that was about to launch its own breakfast television service as a pre-emptive strike to de-stabilise the new IBA contractor, TV-AM.

In any event, all this was "embarrassingly reversed the next day", as the trade press put it. Having argued in its evidence to Hunt for cable to be regulated by the IBA, the BBC now chose to welcome the Cable Authority. Not surprisingly, it also approved the ban on pay-per-view which Hunt proposed – "for the time being", the BBC noted – and the must-carry rule. For some unexplained reason, the BBC saw "great difficulties in implementing" the recommendation on non-exclusive major sporting events. Nor was it persuaded that commitments made during the licensing process could be enforced, declining to believe "that advance assurances made in seeking a franchise are a valid safeguard – experience has shown they are of little value".

It was the BBC's Director-General, Alasdair Milne, who drew the crucial distinction which perhaps explained the BBC's curious posture. Subscription television was not wrong in itself – after all, the BBC would be operating a subscription service on DBS. Satellite was "available potentially to everyone", by individual choice: but access to cable was determined by where the operators chose to install. The BBC expected only 50–60% of the country to be cabled – and even that at a cost of £3–6 billion – and only 50–60% take-up within those areas: figures, by the way, which in practice the cable industry has come nowhere near to achieving.

"It is for this reason," said the BBC, "that regulation is important – to prevent a service to the minority from limiting the choice available to the majority. Regulation is crucial because without it cable could damage and perhaps destroy whole areas of public service broadcasting and with it the variety, scope, quality and balance which such broadcasting currently represents".

The BBC was worried about the absence of quotas – "if foreign material is allowed in freely, the temptation to carry it in preference to home-produced material will be strong". Milne put it brutally: "to imagine that it is possible to buy additional American programmes to the ones we are already enjoying *and* maintain the broadcasting standards we are used to is tantamount to not being in the real world".

And even with UK material, there were still the dangers of siphoning or pushing up costs. Bill Cotton, the managing director designate of the DBS service, deployed yet again the familiar arguments against allowing cable to compete directly with ITV and the BBC. In stark contrast with Hugh Greene's dismissive attitude to ITV at the time of Pilkington, Cotton embraced ITV within the public service approach: "as a duopoly, we only compete for the attention of our audience, not for our income: we therefore can confidently commission and schedule minority programmes".

By contrast, "derestricted cable would introduce a service that would by its nature try to cream off the popular end of programming and have no requirement in terms of quality or indeed choice. Derestricted cable allowed to run riot in the area of popular programming will dilute the available material, therefore the audiences, and therefore the income to the point eventually when there will be nobody interested, or indeed able to invest, in quality programmes made for the domestic market". Moreover, "there is a limit that can be paid for sport [by the BBC] unless once again it is ripped away from the principle of being available to all and siphoned off to a cable sports ghetto for which people would have to pay extra".

These sentiments would re-emerge with much fuller force in the 1990s, in connection with the satellite service, Sky: but because in 1982 the BBC had its own satellite ambitions, it could only attack cable subscription services, and then only because of their geographical exclusiveness. The BBC argued that its satellite subscription service would simply act as an extension of its free-to-air channels, offering feature films prior to their network release, international programmes, news, archive programmes and repeats. Yet in its own evidence to Hunt it had acknowledged that top sport might be featured: "The aspirations of sporting promoters and film producers for a better return could be met through the channels soon to be available on DBS".

"DBS channels," said the BBC, "need not disenfranchise viewers either on geographical or technical grounds. It was the appeal of their universality – the ability of everyone from Brighton to the Butt of Lewis to acquire additional services firstly by the acquisition of a receiving dish and if he so chose, by the payment of a subscription – that attracted the BBC to DBS in the first instance. The ability to pay a little more offers all viewers the enrichment of their choice without the unwelcome social divisiveness that cable must produce". Rupert Murdoch could not have put it better himself.

The BBC had eloquently told Hunt that "if cable becomes symbolic of what Mayfair can have but Brixton cannot, what Metropolitan Man may enjoy but Rural Man is denied, then one more social tension will be generated in an uneasy age. Wideband cable is not likely to make economic sense outside the larger cities and towns, or even the affluent suburbs of some cities. So yet another shadow of social divisiveness may fall across our communities".

Hunt was unimpressed by the BBC's sophistic distinctions, and simply ignored them. He found allies such as the Conservative backbencher, Sir Philip Goodhart, who reminded the Cassandras in a Commons debate that "in civilisation's long history, the greatest single decline in cultural, aesthetic and philosophical standards was produced by the printing press".

Hunt had critics from the right. They felt he had fudged the issues of principle, failing to understand the underlying precepts of economic theory and consumer choice, or to explain the limits he put on cable's potential. "The Hunt Report can be searched in vain," said Veljanovski and Bishop, "for a convincing reason why the industry should be regulated...nowhere is it stated why the local monopoly of cable operators should be controlled". In terms of major sports contracts, "Hunt gives no convincing reason why

BBC and ITV should not pay the full market value for the rights to these events". As for foreign ownership, that it is "unacceptable to whom, and why, in terms of the costs and benefits, is not explained...since the investment required will be both large and risky, and since US capital has far more experience of this form of investment, the harmful consequences may be substantial".

Despite all this, Veljanovski and Bishop had to acknowledge the significance of Hunt's findings: they marked "a sharp break with 60 years of government policy designed to restrict competition in broadcasting". That the government had broadly endorsed the Report on publication "effectively jettisoned the principles upon which the British broadcasting system had been based since its inception...the era of 'rationed TV' subject to public operation and extensive regulation will be over".

Other commentators agreed, though with regret rather than enthusiasm. Lord Annan, far from repenting his description of cable as a parasite, predicted "a flood of trash and porn", if US experience was a guide. He congratulated Lord Hunt for steering between the Home Office and the Department of Industry in the manner of a master civil servant, but for him "the drift of the Report is clear: broadcasting authorities are passing into history".

The *Daily Telegraph* described cable's de-regulated status as "unprecedented in British broadcasting practice". What *The Guardian* saw as unprecedented was the swiftness and fogginess of the political process of which Hunt was a part. Michael Tracey also noted the "incredible speed" at which "the proponents of public service broadcasting" had suffered "a sizeable defeat". "The priesthood," he said, "will painfully come to realise that the congregation has taken over and life will never be quite the same again".

This was a theme to which Hunt himself turned in the Guildhall Lecture he gave soon after publication. Mischievously, he quoted from the Guildhall Lecture by Hugh Greene ten years earlier: "the future of broadcasting in this country is not going to be radically affected by wired systems at any period one can foresee". Hunt's riposte to Greene was: "remember the video recorder". The rapid rise in rentals and purchases of pre-recorded videos supported the findings of the National Consumer Council that 41% of viewers were dissatisfied with what was available on the three channels. "The voice of the consumer has not yet been heard," he said.

Greene was actually chairing Hunt's lecture, and could not resist seeking the last word: "which would be the greater disaster for this country: if cable TV failed – which is quite possible – or if it succeeded...which is also quite possible?"

Six months after Hunt was published, a government White Paper adopted virtually all his recommendations, save only that licences would run for twelve years, advertising would face restrictions in extent, and pay-per-view would after all be permitted, though only for material not yet being broadcast. The new Cable Authority would have as its first director – the secretary of the Hunt Committee, Jon Davey. It had taken all of twenty years for Channel 4 to emerge from first blueprint in the Pilkington Report to the reality of launch in November 1982. Now, in less than twenty months, the way had been cleared for the much-heralded cable revolution. Paradoxically, it did not happen.

The government was primarily to blame. For instance, it attempted to impose its own preferred technology on the cable franchises, which proved counter-productive. The insistence on telephony being provided by BT or Mercury deprived cable operators of a competitive edge – Veljanovski and Bishop had no doubt that "so short-sighted a policy will reduce the long-term employment prospects cable expansion can offer Britain". Their predictions as to the ill-effects of excluding American capital proved equally well-founded. When the government changed its capital allowance tax policies, UK investment in cable ground to a halt. Only when foreign ownership was allowed, and cable was permitted to offer telephony in competition with BT – but BT forbidden to offer entertainment – did cable's expansion gather pace.

Even then, a crucial ingredient proved to be the availability of entertainment services delivered by satellite. But not by the BBC. In satellite, too, the government crucially miscalculated. The BBC's DBS plans proved to be too costly to fund. An attempt to shoehorn the BBC into an alliance with ITV and other commercial interests through the so-called Club of 21 quickly collapsed. ITV's launch of a Superchannel satellite service targeted at European viewers failed just as swiftly. Only when one of the two ITV companies that refused to join Superchannel – Thames – solved the satellite conundrum through an investment in a Luxembourg venture called SES Astra was a clear course successfully navigated. And then it was Rupert Murdoch who led the way, with cable only finally setting sail in the wake of his ambition.

Meanwhile, Hunt himself had been overtaken by the far more formidable Peacock Report. Here could be found full-blooded endorsement of the consumer-led, rather than producer-driven, approach to broadcasting. No-one could accuse Peacock of lack of logic or economic understanding. But if the full impact of the Hunt Report was inadvertently muffled by the government that had commissioned it, with hindsight we can see that it changed the political perception of the structure of broadcasting as decisively as technology was changing the consumer's perception. How much further Peacock took this process is the subject of the next lecture: but it is from the Hunt Report four years earlier that we must date the decisive shift in the way broadcasting was to be regulated and managed.

[5]
Peacock

9 March 1999

Whose words are these?

> The BBC and the regulated ITV system have done far better, in mimicking the effects of a true consumer market, than any purely laissez-faire system, financed by advertising, could have done under conditions of spectrum shortage.

Does that come from the Annan Report? The Labour Party? The BBC or IBA? Let's hear more.

> We would go further: they have provided packages of programmes to audiences at remarkably low cost...the intertwining of information, education and entertainment has broadened the horizons of great numbers of viewers and listeners...the notion of cross-fertilisation of programme categories is inherent in BBC practice – and in ITV practice, too – and of great value...all that is in accord with the Reithian tradition.

Pilkington perhaps? A final clue.

> It is, indeed, important that...we do not, prematurely, dismantle or destroy the 'packaged' terrestrial broadcasting services that give good value today. The practice of providing a mixed diet at low cost is one that we wish to see continued. It is, in our view, compatible with the recommendations...for future funding of the BBC through subscription.

These are, of course, quotations from the Peacock Report, the last of the post-war committees of enquiry into broadcasting that are dealt with in this lecture series. If some people today find all but the last of those words quoted surprising – half-remembering the notoriety of Peacock as a free market manifesto – then imagine the dismay such sentiments must have caused in the hearts of those hard-line Tories who had seen the Peacock Committee as the chosen instrument of bringing the BBC to heel.

The election of 1979 that installed Mrs Thatcher in Downing Street was to have profound effects on British broadcasting. She had little patience with entrenched oligopolies, particularly if they failed to share her firmly held views. The warning signs were there from the beginning, with the first outburst of ministerial outrage over a BBC Panorama team filming an IRA unit operating a roadblock in the Ulster village of Carrickmore – a story that broke in October 1979 on a day the cabinet was due to discuss the licence fee.

It was in attacks on the licence fee that hostility to the BBC found expression. *The Times* ran a series of anti-BBC leaders – open, of course, to the charge that its views conveniently fitted the commercial interests of its proprietor, Rupert Murdoch, who operated the BBC's loss-making satellite competitor, Sky Television.

No similar accusation could be directed at the Adam Smith Institute, a right-wing think tank. Their 1984 publication, *The Omega File*, condemned the licence fee for its failure to relate the requirement to pay to consumer preference. The BBC was guaranteed its income "almost regardless of the quality or content of its broadcasting".

It was the Falklands War, which triggered an explosion of anger amongst Conservative MPs in protest at the BBC's even-handed treatment of British and Argentine information sources. The Corporation's chairman, George Howard, and director-general, Alasdair Milne, were given a tremendous roasting at the House of Commons.

The twin thrusts of the attack converged in 1985. The BBC's vice-chairman at the time, Lord Rees-Mogg, a Thatcher appointee, was aware that Conservatives saw the BBC as arrogant and no longer impartial – or perhaps too impartial! He believed it would be only a matter of time before "politicians would get fed up with the BBC behaving in this way and would start to cut it down to size – and indeed they did: the Peacock Committee was set up with just such a view".

Leon Brittan, who had been Willie Whitelaw's skilful Minister of State during the creation of Channel Four and was now Home Secretary himself, announced an inquiry, to be chaired by Professor Alan Peacock, to the House of Commons on March 27th, 1985. The Labour Party was quick to pounce. "As right-wing as can be found," was how one backbench MP described Peacock, who was a prominent liberal economist. Another MP insinuated that "this inquisition" was expected to come to the "foregone conclusion that there should be advertising at least on BBC1 and BBC2". Brittan responded by pointing out that Peacock had for two years been an adviser to the previous Labour government and by denying that there was "a subtle plot to force advertising on the BBC". But the Committee's narrow terms of reference fed opposition suspicions.

For Peacock's status was actually as chairman of "the Committee on Financing the BBC", not one investigating broadcasting as a whole. The terms Brittan announced to the Commons overwhelmingly addressed whether and how advertising and sponsorship should be used to fund the BBC – the only other brief reference being to "securing income from the consumer other than through the licence fee".

Understandably, Labour's shadow Home Secretary, Gerald Kaufman, denounced Peacock as the wrong inquiry – "an inquiry almost solely confined to the effects of the introduction of advertising and options for advertising is unacceptable". Brittan pointed out that sponsorship was also mentioned – scarcely a point to deflect Kaufman – and that the phrase "other than through the licence fee" might include subscription: a nugget of information that all MPs ignored as Kaufman grandly committed his party to a brace of binding policy commitments.

> There are no circumstances in which a Labour Government will permit advertising on either BBC television or radio. Professor Peacock must take that into account. A Labour Government will also phase out the licence so that no retirement pensioners will have to pay for a television licence. I make that commitment clearly and firmly on behalf of the Labour Party and the next Government of this country.

Twelve years are a long time in politics, so such pledges can be assumed no longer to apply. After all, under Attlee, the Labour Party once committed itself to abolishing ITV. Leon Brittan, well-prepared, simply contented himself with pointing out to Kaufman that to absolve pensioners from the licence fee would cost the BBC £325 million a year.

Brittan also assured the Commons that Peacock would be free to draw his own conclusions. However, this conciliatory note was somewhat undermined a few weeks later when the Committee's other six members were named. They included an industrialist and philosopher of confirmed right-of-centre views, and, to general astonishment, the Home Secretary's own older brother, Sam Brittan, a noted liberal economist and *Financial Times* columnist. The trade paper, Broadcast, described Sam Brittan as the Committee's intellectual powerhouse. As a whole, the Committee looked even more stacked than its chairman's identity originally suggested.

In fact, it was another action by Leon Brittan that caused the BBC most initial difficulty. He had timed his announcement of Peacock's appointment just four days before the BBC's three-year licence settlement was due to expire. The BBC had been pressing for its £46 colour licence fee to rise to £65 – a rate well ahead of inflation, but which the BBC sought to justify in a brochure hubristically entitled "the best bargain in Britain". Critics were quick to point out that bargains were usually something you could choose to leave on the shelf. The Home Secretary was amongst those unconvinced, conceding only a £58 fee, to last for at least two years – depending on exactly when and what Peacock reported.

Peacock took a dim view of this old-fashioned haggle. To live within the £58 limit, the Home Secretary had invited the BBC to undertake economies and re-organisation: "none," noted Peacock, "was described as potentially disastrous to the BBC...all these measures seemed to us to be extremely worthwhile, but we ask ourselves why they had not been adopted before".

Peacock went further. "In granting finance to the BBC, the Government has to rely on the BBC for the information which will influence its decision. However, the BBC has never been asked to relate its requirements to target 'outputs' and to justify these. The process of budgeting for the BBC's 'needs' and the monitoring of its use of its funds seems to be of the crudest kind".

The next point could have come straight from The Omega Report. "It has become increasingly clear that a vital element is left out of the discussion. The consumer has a direct interest in the amount of the fixed charge payable irrespective of the amount of his viewing or listening, but has no power to control what the charge should be...the sole direct source of information on the costs to be covered by the charge is the state broadcasting monopoly, which is an interested party. Therefore, there can be no guarantee that the fixed charge is the minimum compatible with the provision of a given quantum of broadcasting services. The incentives normally provided by competition are lacking".

The Committee was unimpressed by the BBC's regular pledges to greater efficiency as monitored by firms of accountants, noting, rather, a tendency "to take refuge in the findings of the Peat Marwick 'Value for Money' review of its activities". Even this generally favourable report from Peat Marwick left Peacock complaining that the BBC had supplied no useful data to his Committee, and had "ignored a very important set of recommendations about the use of 'performance indicators'" that the document had put forward.

The Committee's view of the BBC had not been improved by Alasdair Milne's performance at the all-day open session Peacock organised in London half way through his deliberations. The Report cited – clearly disapprovingly – Milne's view that "broadcasting is a process of scattering and thus sowing seed far and wide...some will fall on stony ground and some on fertile ground...broadcasting further means that the sower waits to see what grows" – an attitude whereby, in Peacock's words, "the viewer's main function is to react to a set of choices determined by the broadcasting institutions".

Fortunately for the BBC, this was the limit of Peacock's adverse comments. He rejected, as Annan had before him, the suggestion that BBC television and radio be divided – "although the range and quality of BBC radio programmes might well be enhanced by separation from television, it appears that the BBC is better retained as a single unit". The reasons offered for this decision were skimpy, but perhaps what was most remarkable about the Peacock Report was the intellectual process by which it stood back from the institutional weaknesses of the BBC and concentrated on the broadcasting environment in which it operated. "It would have been tempting, " said the Report, "to confine ourselves to a limited examination of the case for and against the introduction of advertising on the BBC...[but] before we can devise guidelines for the finance of broadcasting, we have to specify its purposes".

Peacock's view of those purposes was far removed from that of previous Committees. The question he asked himself would have stuck in Pilkington's throat: "how can British broadcasting be financed in such a way as to bring the greatest enjoyment and pleasure to as many viewers and listeners as possible while at the same time fulfilling some public service obligation?" Peacock's answer? "The fundamental aim of broadcasting policy should in our view be to enlarge both the freedom and the choice of the consumer and the opportunities available to programme makers to offer alternative wares to the public". Lord Annan was quick to note that this definition virtually abolished the previously central role of the broadcasting authorities around which he had created his own Report.

Peacock was by no means unaware that his Committee's very existence challenged received wisdom. Wherever he went, he found "expressions of amazement – even from NBC and ABC in the United States – that the British should be thinking of changing their system, which is almost universally admired". The first question the Committee addressed was: "Why is it right to look at a system of financing the BBC which has been in operation so long and which has been endorsed by every committee to review it?" Their justification was that "no political decision as complex and detailed as that which determines the structure of broadcasting can be right for all time – it must be reviewed in the light of changing circumstances".

What had changed for the BBC was that the licence fee had lost its buoyancy. For over sixty years, rises in the number of licence fee payers – first for radio, then for combined radio and television, then for colour television – had allowed BBC revenue to grow faster than the nominal rate of the licence fee itself. But as colour licences reached saturation point, increases in the cost of the licence were the only means to maintain the BBC's spending power in parity with ITV.

The BBC's own evidence to Peacock noted that there had been six increases in the licence fee in the previous ten years, compared with seven in the previous fifty-three years. "In political circles generally," conceded the BBC, this "has brought about some loss of confidence in the long-term durability of the licence fee system". Having described the licence fee to Annan as the least unsatisfactory means of funding itself, the BBC depicted it to Peacock as "for the time being, still the most effective means of financing its various services in what is inevitably an imperfect world".

For Peacock, the problem was that this loss of buoyancy in BBC income was accompanied by rapid growth in the advertising revenue that fuelled ITV. If a primary objective was to keep a balance between the two systems, instability was inevitable. Moreover, the growth of cable and satellite would speed this de-stabilisation: "to consider the BBC as if it will continue with something like half of the small number of channels available is to fail to grasp the nature of changes which are already taking place and whose intensification seems irresistible".

In any case, Peacock had a rooted objection to the parity model. Like Annan, but for different reasons, he disliked what he called "the comfortable duopoly". "There is good reason," he said, "to question whether a regulated duopoly does promote or could be designed to promote the welfare of viewers and listeners". Furthermore, "economic analysis of duopoly situations does not offer much support for the view that if the duopoly is stable the interests of the consumer rather than the producers will be paramount".

He pointed to the elaborate system of cross-subsidies – from the centre to the regions, and from high-audience, low-cost programmes to high-cost, low-audience ones – as well as the absence of incentives to be cost-conscious. He observed, witheringly, that the BBC and ITV "direct a good deal of their effort to enhancing their reputation with fellow professionals".

Research commissioned by Peacock established that, measured by numbers of international awards, British television was "far and away the best in the world". Yet according to a survey carried out for the National Consumer Council, 45% of the public were dissatisfied with British television, and only 46% satisfied. "All our experience of measuring consumers' attitudes," said the NCC, "show that you can normally expect about 75-80% to say they are satisfied with a service, whatever it is: 46% satisfaction is a very low figure".

Whilst accepting that secure funding and mutual tolerance of parity in audience share allowed the broadcasters "peace to plan" and viewers "a wider variety of programmes than commercial considerations would dictate", Peacock could not but help observe that "paradoxically, the status quo, given its requirement of retaining existing funding proportions, represents an unstable situation". Told that "the biggest headache from the BBC's point of view is maintaining its spending power in relation to ITV companies", he concluded that the licence fee would be placed under intolerable strain in trying to match the steady growth in advertising – "consumer resistance would be bound to grow if the fixed proportion rule were paramount, and changes in the method of raising the licence fee would serve at best a cosmetic purpose".

Keeping up with the ITV Joneses in any case carried the inherent objection that it transferred into the whole of broadcasting the specific inefficiencies within the ITV companies. Even the ingenious notion of funding the BBC's additional annual needs out of ITV's levy did not address this fundamental problem. Peacock noted that the Treasury's proceeds from the ITV levy were flat, despite the rising curve of ITV revenue. Whether the levy was charged on turnover or profits, ITV's monopoly of advertising "does not encourage these companies to minimise costs...their levels of remuneration are higher than is necessary to retain their professional labour (ie monopoly profits are shared between employees and shareholders) and this puts pressure on the BBC to follow wage increases granted by the independent television companies".

As a result, in general "the broadcasting industry was wasteful of resources through over-manning and self-indulgent working practices...whatever method of finance was appropriate for financing the BBC, the public had a right to expect that broadcasting services should be provided at the lowest possible cost compatible with the provision of a service of high quality". Peacock observed that although the BBC appeared to be more cost-effective than ITV, independent producers seemed more efficient than either – an observation that was to have dramatic consequences.

Whilst admiring – as we have seen – some of the outcomes of public service broadcasting as provided by the duopoly arrangements, Peacock felt its weaknesses outweighed them. There was an "absence of true consumer sovereignty", the system was "vulnerable to political pressure and vulnerable to trade union and other special interest groups", the ITV franchise process was "near impossible" to be run fairly, and there was the "endemic weakness in the control of cost or pursuit of efficiency". His verdict on the old system was damning: "even if it could by a superhuman effort of governmental regulation be preserved into the 21st century, it would be wrong in principle to seek to do so".

So what could replace it? True to his remit, Peacock addressed the issue of advertising on the BBC exhaustively – and decisively rejected it. In all, the Committee received 843 submissions; 658 were on the subject of advertising. The advertisers themselves acknowledged the deep improbability of there being enough revenue to replace the licence fee and sustain commercial radio and television. At best, the BBC's requirements over and above a frozen licence fee might be met by absorbing £100 million a year of the natural annual growth in advertising. Some advertisers felt this could be done without damaging ITV and ILR. But these commercial broadcasters submitted that they would be driven into the red if the BBC took as much as two minutes of advertising every hour.

The BBC, of course, had no desire to be what they called "a little bit pregnant", suffering all the pressures of being dependent on advertising, whilst still facing regular negotiations with governments keen to reduce the licence fee rather than just freeze it. Peacock was conscious of the fate of New Zealand's equivalent of the BBC, which had been induced to take advertising as a 10% supplement to its licence revenue, and had soon found itself 70% dependent on it.

Peacock commissioned a series of specialist economic analyses which persuaded him that demand for advertising was simply not elastic enough to take up all the slots that a fully commercial system would offer, without the price dropping sharply. One pair of experts predicted that total advertising revenue might even fall. Peacock noted that "at present the IBA is helped in its regulatory function by the fact that a low audience share for ITV would (if our econometrics are correct) increase ITV revenues since advertisers would need to advertise more to reach a given level of audience size and the ensuing competition for advertising slots would push up the prices".

The message for Peacock was clear. Competition for advertising revenue, whether limited or full-blooded, and however gradually introduced, would ultimately force the BBC to modify its schedule: "range and quality would become vulnerable to the need to maximise audiences; and much of the good drama and current affairs output would become starved of funding – a narrowing of the range of programmes on both BBC1 and ITV appears almost inevitable at an early stage". Nor was Peacock persuaded that sponsorship could offer more than "a modest supplement to BBC funds".

Research commissioned by Peacock showed that 62% of the public thought it "a good idea" to substitute advertising for the licence fee. But this finding was discounted, because, said Peacock, "those in favour of replacing the licence fee with advertising were chiefly of the view that this would not affect programme quality": and 83% were opposed to advertising if it would reduce programme quality, which Peacock was confident would be the outcome.

There was a deeper problem. Peacock had become increasingly attracted, not just by the notion of consumer welfare, but of consumer sovereignty. This happy state could only be achieved when all households were connected to a common carrier of virtually unlimited numbers of channels and programmes, allowing all providers free or low-cost access to the transmission system, and all consumers the freedom to choose from whatever was on offer on a pay-as-you-go basis.

A crucial distinction he drew was between an advertiser-funded broadcasting system and this consumer-driven version. "It follows from our concept of consumer sovereignty that we reject the commercial laissez-faire model, which is based on a small number of broadcasters competing to sell audiences to advertisers". So Peacock was able to reject replacing the licence fee with advertising, not just because of its effect on the BBC and on broadcasting standards generally, but because of its inferiority on economic and philosophical grounds, too.

The phrase most often used to describe Peacock's vision of the future was electronic publishing. Its chief exponent was the economics journalist, Peter Jay, who had first advanced the notion in an article in *The Times* in 1970, expanded it in an open memorandum to the Annan Committee in 1977 (who politely praised it but then ignored it as too idealistic), and fully elaborated it in his 1981 MacTaggart Lecture at the Edinburgh International Television Festival. Jay wrote to Peacock and spoke eloquently at the open day. His advocacy struck a ready chord, not least with Sam

Brittan, who was particularly attracted by the freedom of speech argument.

The first sustained passage in the Peacock Report gave a strong indication of its concerns. The evils of censorship – embodied in the Inquisition, the Star Chamber and the Stationers' Company, with its 120-year long monopoly on printing – were contrasted with the champions of liberty: Milton, Macaulay, Wilkes and the First Amendment.

The Committee argued that "electronic publishing is founded on the proposition that communication is an activity which does not normally require government intervention...what brought government and the law-makers into the picture was the simple fact of broadcasting technology". We now suffered the twin defects of restricted entry and "massive control and regulation...[through] an elaborate series of formal and informal codes".

By contrast, "rather before the end of the century, Mr Jay argues, it would be possible using fibre-optic technology to create a grid connecting every household in the country, whereby the nation's viewers could simultaneously watch as many different programmes as the nation's readers can simultaneously read different books, magazines and newspapers".

Peacock did not entirely endorse this somewhat utopian scenario, pointing out that "satellite technology...is in its infancy" and that "it could be well into the 21st century before there is a heavy penetration of wideband transmission capability into the national communications network down to the subscriber's premises". The Committee noted the low take-up of cable, asserted that "at present cable is an uncertain investment" and looked to BT (British Telecom) – whose chairman, Sir George Jefferson, was an influential witness – to help build the national network in return for being allowed to offer the entertainment services from which it had been excluded in the hope of encouraging the growth of cable.

Whether by cable, direct broadcasting by satellite, BT or otherwise, Peacock believed the fully interconnected society would eventually materialise: "we hope that as broadcasting moves towards the full maturity of the sophisticated market, the justification for general restrictions imposed in the first century of broadcasting to reflect both the scarcity of the spectrum and the novelty of the medium will wither away…the end of all censorship arrangements would be a sign that broadcasting had come to age, like publishing three centuries ago…pre-publication censorship has no place in a free society".

Peacock did not imagine consumer sovereignty as a passive expression of "static wants" – rather as a "discovery mechanism" in which "viewers and listeners are the best ultimate judges of their own interests". But what he had no interest in was "compulsory uplift" – if people "still make for junk food, that is their privilege in a free society".

What Peacock was forced to concede, however, was that his ideal system lay far in the future. He had to find an intellectual, economic and practical link between that future and the present. What he seized upon was the intermediate technology of subscription. For Peacock, "the whole subject of subscription technology brings with it the opportunity for viewers and listeners to pay for what they want to receive and to have a much greater choice of programmes…subscription technology can on the one hand simply be used as a more convenient device for collecting the licence fee; on the other hand it can open the door to an almost infinite number of channels or programmes or indeed many other facilities – banking, direct mail ordering, etc".

When the Peacock Report was published, the notion of subscription as a mechanism for funding the BBC was widely ridiculed. Few had openly advocated it to Peacock, apart from myself and the National Consumers Council. Yet it had a long pedigree amongst economists, with notable papers published in

1962, 1968 and 1982 – one written by a former deputy chairman of the IBA.

What commentators appeared to have missed was that the idea of subscription featured heavily in the evidence from both the BBC and the Labour Party. The BBC, in acknowledging the deficiencies of the licence fee, explicitly said: "perhaps the most beguiling prospect for future alternative or ancillary funding lies in the direction of subscription".

The BBC's preference, of course, was for all channels to be scrambled: "such a system would end all prospect of evasion at a stroke, introduce an automatic additional payment for additional sets and, most important, eliminate unfair competition between ITV, still perceived as free, and 'subscriber' BBC".

Whether or not as a result of a tip-off about the Committee's thinking, the Labour Party told Peacock: "there appear to be strong reasons for suspecting that subscription might be advanced as a likely medium term solution to the problem of financing the BBC…there is evidence (notably from an IBA study in 1984) to suggest that demand for BBC programmes would mean that subscription could be charged at a considerably higher level than the existing licence fee". Moreover, "a subscription system would ensure the independence of the BBC from Government control and censorship".

Yet the Labour Party opposed subscription, because it breached what it saw as two important principles. The first was that all services should be provided universally at a fixed price, which seems less a principle than a description of the crudest possible form of subscription. The second was that it might eliminate cross-subsidies between services – presumably between BBC1 and BBC2, or between BBC television and BBC radio, but the Labour Party did not specify, nor explain why the cross-subsidies would disappear, let alone why they constituted a principle. Indeed, supporters of subscription argued that the subsidies implicit in the licence fee system were not entirely welcome:

single-set households subsidised multi-set households, the honest licence payers subsidised the dishonest licence evaders, the poor paid the same fee as the rich, private households subsidised hotels, and those within easy reach of transmitters subsidised those in remote areas.

Labour's greatest worry was that subscription services might not be universally taken up, and so lead to some kind of social exclusion. But, as Peacock pointed out, such exclusion was voluntary. "Optional subscription clearly breaches" the principle of universality, but it adds "an extra opportunity (opting out)" – and "government regulation of price or even quality of service...is one possible answer to the claim that subscription television is inherently divisive".

Nor did Peacock accept the argument that "types of programming for which consumer demand is weak" might be squeezed out in a subscription service. This was a point made twenty years earlier by an American economist, Jora Minasian: "a subscription system can be expected to yield a more diversified programme menu than an advertising system because the former enables individuals, by concentrating their dollar votes, to overcome the 'unpopularity' of their tastes". And as Peacock had already noted, the licence fee could not register intensity of viewer preference at all.

Peacock was encouraged by the BBC's apparent open-mindedness: "the BBC evidence...makes clear that subscription is feasible...there is at least some support in the BBC evidence for a subscription system (although there is more than one view in the Corporation) and a good deal of confidence within the Corporation in its ability to sell its services directly under such a system".

What also struck Peacock was how vulnerable the BBC was to licence evasion. It did not control collection, which lay in the expensive hands of the Post Office. Estimated licence defaulters numbered 1.6 million households, yet just 85,000 evaders had been convicted in the previous year. Their average fine was only £7 above the level of the licence fee. Moreover, Peacock's researchers pointed out that the official evasion figures missed the clear discrepancy between the number of monochrome television sets estimated to be in use and the much larger number of monochrome licences held – suggesting more than half a million further defaulting households.

Peacock could see that encryption of BBC services would effectively halt licence evasion: but the attractions of subscription went beyond that. As two-set and even three-set homes grew in number, the possibility of restoring the missing buoyancy in BBC finances beckoned. It was true that an encrypted signal could be fed to more than one set, but such sets could only allow the same programme to be viewed at any one time. If different sets were to be used for viewing different services, each would need a decoder: "subscription television thus has the potential of raising extra revenue from multiple-set owners". Peacock even took care to note that a BBC funded by subscription "would preserve the long-established principle of British broadcasting that each major provider of television can count on its own distinctive source of revenue".

Peacock conducted some fairly crude research into public willingness to pay for the BBC voluntarily, but had to admit that "the numbers are awkwardly inconsistent, and we cannot place much reliance on them". He estimated that take-up of the BBC on subscription would be in the 45–95% range – not very helpful – with the likely outcome being 75–80%, leaving the BBC dependent on multi-set buoyancy to avoid either a subscription rate higher than the licence fee or a cut in quality of service. Nonetheless, so persuaded was he of the virtues of subscription that he recommended the switch to it be subsidised: "there is a strong case for the Government or the BBC paying for or providing cheap finance for the decoders...this would be an investment in the broadcasting market analogous, for instance, to investment in roads".

He went further. The number one recommendation in his report was to copy the French and Italians and make compulsory the installation in every new television set of a special peritelevision socket. This would increase the cost of new televisions but greatly reduce the manufacturing cost of decoders that would plug into the sockets.

Meanwhile, Peacock fully acknowledged that, if his perfect market was a distant stage three of the process, even stage two – subscription – was some years distant: though in his view "likely to start well before the end of the century". Meanwhile, in stage one, the BBC needed stability, and the damaging effects of ITV's entrenched inefficiency had to be curbed. This led to a flurry of proposals at the end of the Report, which bore little relation to the fifteen questions in the consultation document issued by the Committee at the start of their deliberations.

The final chapter – number 12 – of the Peacock Report contained his conclusions and recommendations. One can only assume it was written well after the rest of the Report and, indeed, after an intense debate amongst the members. The truth is that many of the ideas introduced at this stage had only the sketchiest connection with the previous chapters – for example, the call for 40% of all television output to be provided, within ten years, by independent producers rather than the broadcasters themselves.

This signalled a tremendous victory for the independent lobby, which had first emerged as a force only five years earlier during the shaping of Channel 4. They argued that they represented diversity and lower costs – both calculated to appeal to Peacock, who pronounced: "the requirements for in-house production are at the root of union restrictive practices". ITV and the BBC using independents – and not just Channel 4 – would "increase competition and multiply sources of supply", as well as relieving the plight of the independents themselves, who were "constrained by their limited market and their virtual dependence on a single monopoly buyer".

To justify this line of argument, Peacock referred his readers back
to paragraphs 71-74 of his Report. Unfortunately, these paragraphs deal only with the structure of Channel 4, and make no reference to independent producers at all. Similarly, the opening paragraph of Chapter 12, claiming that "much of the unpopularity of the licence fee arises from the annual lump sum nature of the payment, and the burden it inflicts on the poor", refers us back to paragraph 209 – which has nothing to say about the annual lump sum. It was, in fact, the BBC in its own evidence to Peacock that made this assertion. Paragraphs 439-448 are then cited to justify saying: "the evidence we have received from public opinion surveys shows a degree of public willingness to pay directly for BBC programmes and services" – which is only true if you do not examine the word "degree" too carefully.

That the conclusions were so evidently put together in a hurry led some commentators to claim, as details of the last-minute arguments started to leak, that this was a "Committee desperate for something radical to say". A fairer comment would be that the recommendations, unlike the Report, followed no logical pattern. They attempted to create a pathway to what the Report called stage two, in preparation for a stage three in the distant future, but with most recommended measures concentrated in stage one.

So recommendation two simply absolved BBC television of any requirement to accept advertisements before the advent of subscription; but recommendation seven gave the BBC the option to privatise radios 1 and 2 and local radio. Indeed five of the seven members of the Committee would have imposed such privatisation, in the belief that it would strengthen the commercial radio sector and do little damage to the BBC – saving annual running costs and providing a handy lump sum. The five even favoured a worker-management buy-out, though offering not a glimmer of evidence to support such a proposal.

Meanwhile, the licence fee would be index-linked to retail prices, the BBC would be given control of collection, pensioners drawing supplementary pension in households wholly dependent on a pension would be exempt from the licence fee, and a £10 radio licence would be charged for car radios – despite the fact that this very notion had been discarded in the body of the Report! Again, if we look back at the BBC's own evidence to Peacock, we can see the origin of the idea. Noting that the radio licence fee had been abolished in 1971, because collection costs were 25% of revenue, but when there were already a million radios in cars, the BBC noted regretfully: "fifteen years on we must ask whether total abolition might have damaged the BBC".

This combination of measures Peacock thought would leave the BBC roughly neutral in financial terms. His preference for RPI-linking rather than using a broadcast costs index was that "this would put some pressure on the BBC to exploit its revenue-earning potential more forcefully and to think more carefully before embarking on peripheral activities far removed from its core obligations". The BBC was already sensitive to such implicit criticism, and had promised – once the DBS venture had collapsed – to keep its hands off cable and satellite – "the BBC seeks no significant part in these developments...the BBC's claim, both for position and for funds, concerns its role as a continuing provider of new programmes for the whole nation".

To open up broadcasting a little, Peacock proposed selling off the night-time hours ITV and the BBC were not using – again, citing the BBC's evidence (in support of its own commercial proposal to download material at night for recording on videos) that "the marginal running costs of the BBC1 network were less than £500 an hour". More importantly, and most controversially, a majority of the Peacock committee recommended auctioning the ITV licences to the highest of those bidders who passed a quality threshold – a proposal designed to replace the featherbedding of the levy and introduce efficient use of spectrum, in equal measure.

In addition, Peacock called for restrictions preventing non-EEC ownership of cable franchises to be removed, all restrictions on pay television to be lifted, and Channel 4 to be allowed the option of selling its own advertising, so giving up its dependence on ITV funding. As a final flourish, in anticipation of broadcast content eventually being subject simply to the law of the land, Peacock suggested that such legislation as the Obscene Publications Act should no longer exempt broadcasting on the grounds of it being separately regulated.

Peacock was not sure when the transfer to subscription might take place, so he offered a safety net to protect minority programming in stage two. He proposed that a Public Service Broadcasting Council be set up – perhaps funded by the ITV auction proceeds. This would support programmes offering knowledge, culture, criticism and experiment, on radio and television, and would not be confined to any one channel. "If a full broadcasting market is eventually achieved, in which viewers and listeners can express preferences directly, the main role of public service could turn out to be the collective provision...of programmes which viewers and listeners are willing to support in their capacity of taxpayers and voters, but not directly as consumers".

Knowing that the BBC insisted that its public service role covered the full range of programmes – how else could the universal compulsory licence fee be justified? – Peacock anticipated that this idea would not be popular with the broadcasters, who would depict it as an Arts Council ghetto. "The present system is unlikely to last far into the 1990s," warned Peacock. "Past successes... may in the future create a fool's paradise. It is time to recognise the need for public finance for public service programmes...the defenders of the duopoly may unwittingly be the worst enemies of high quality programmes in the arts, current affairs and for specialised tastes". Peacock's rhetoric could not disguise a failure in logic: if subscription funding could be expected to sustain a full range of programming, why was a Public Service Broadcasting Council needed?

No doubt conscious that his 18 recommendations – a mere handful compared with the hundred or more of Beveridge, Pilkington and Annan – could easily be implemented or ignored selectively, Peacock concluded by saying that they were "designed to form part of a coherent strategy…it is not possible to pick and choose at will among them, without destroying the whole thrust". No doubt all chairmen are tempted to similar pieties.

But his final paragraph offered an overview rare in conciseness. "We have neither sought to 'get the BBC off the hook' nor to persecute it. If we had to summarise our conclusion by one slogan (which most of us would not want to do), it would be direct consumer choice rather than continuation of the licence fee. The arrangements we suggest for the latter, though designed to take the heat out of the subject, are designed to bridge the period before subscription becomes practicable. Eventually we hope to reach a position where the mystique is taken out of broadcasting and it becomes no more special than publishing became once the world became used to living with the printing press".

The Peacock Report was published in July 1986. It was greeted with a storm of abuse, anger and derision from broadcasters, regulators, unions, MPs and ministers. Gerald Kaufman described the Report as "ideological dementia" which "should be put in the waste paper basket". A minister was heard to describe Peacock as a "dead duck". There was universal astonishment that Peacock had both declined to re-shape the BBC and then spectacularly exceeded his remit by recommending major surgery on ITV and Channel Four. The IBA predicted that the separate selling of its own advertising would "wreck" Channel 4. One ITV chief, David Plowright of Granada, denouncing the licence auction, quipped that "we have already got one show on the air called *The Price Is Right*". Another, Christopher Bland of LWT, called the auction "a pretty loopy procedure…a Friday afternoon suggestion".

The trade paper, *Broadcast*, called the auction "a shark's charter". With a mixture of scorn and admiration, it noted that "seldom has a government set up a committee with clearer instructions on precisely what it was expected to report...seldom has a committee so disappointed and defied its political masters".

One of *Broadcast's* columnists, Nick Higham – now the BBC's own media correspondent – gave the Report even shorter shrift. "It has brought in from the lunatic fringe two proposals for the organisation of broadcasting which even two years ago would have received scant serious attention from broadcasters or policy-makers. These are the scrambling of broadcast television signals so that they are accessible only to subscribers who have paid for the appropriate decoder, and the auctioning of the broadcasting frequency spectrum". Higham had no doubt of Peacock's fate: "savaged by opposition politicians, dismissed by a patronising Home Secretary as 'stimulating, challenging' and having exceeded its brief, the Committee's Report was shoved unceremoniously into the deepest pigeon-hole the Home Office could find, leaving only a few stray feathers to remind us of its passing".

This dismissive diatribe proved decidedly premature. The Peacock Report may not have been entirely to Mrs Thatcher's taste – she called herself an economic liberal, but freedom of speech attracted her far less – yet she chose to chair the cabinet committee dealing with broadcasting. Soon, the sheer power of Peacock's arguments and Thatcher's will would cut a swathe through the world of television. For this, Peacock can claim much of the credit – or the blame.

With its coloured charts and diagrams, its sophisticated economic analyses, and its emphasis on the centrality of the consumer rather than the broadcaster, the Peacock Report looked, felt and read utterly differently from its predecessors. It was easily the most brilliant of the five such inquiries since the war: but because its focus was primarily on the distant future, it missed much that lay immediately ahead – such as the prospects for a fifth terrestrial channel and the significance of medium-powered satellites. Even Peacock would probably have been surprised to find, just ten years after publication, 30% of the population enjoying access to 50 channels of television.

Yet, at its best, the intensity of his logic and the clarity of his vision dwarf his failings. The reverberations of his Report would be felt for a decade or more, even though his key recommendation – subscription funding – would only achieve its impact through a route he barely anticipated.

In the last lecture of this series – entitled "The Politics of Digital" – I will trace the battle over Peacock, Mrs Thatcher's calculated assault on television, the emergence of satellite as a key force for change, and the attempt to construct a new political rationale for regulating broadcasting within the framework of the digital revolution. And finally, I will try to place in the context of the last fifty years the latest Review Committee, led by Gavyn Davies, whose terms of reference bear a remarkable resemblance to those of Peacock itself.

[6]
After Peacock: The Politics Of Digital

11 March 1999

The Peacock Report, published in July 1986, had been simultaneously bullish and cautious about the future of broadcasting. The technological prospects were alluring, but "any attempt to look ahead should...be governed by caution, humility and by a realistic view of what government policy can achieve". Peacock even tried his one modest attempt at wit. Faced with an inflow of satellite programming, he predicted that "governments would find that, like King Canute, they could not control the waves".

Professor Peacock had reckoned without Margaret Thatcher. Despite a series of embarrassing governmental setbacks in failed attempts to impose industrial preferences on broadcasting, the Prime Minister was still on the warpath. Douglas Hurd's Home Office had signalled, immediately after publication, that the Peacock Report would be consigned "to the long grass". But once Mrs Thatcher herself had taken the chair of the cabinet committee dealing with broadcasting, and brought on board her hard-liners – Lord Young, Norman Tebbit and Nigel Lawson – Hurd found himself outnumbered and outgunned. His most senior broadcasting civil servant, Quentin Thomas, reports having to accommodate the "very close interest" being shown by the Treasury and the Department for Trade and Industry.

By October 1986, Hurd was publicly supporting subscription – it "fits well into the general approach of this government" – and even questioning public service broadcasting – "it cannot chunter on for ever". Mrs Thatcher herself characterised public service broadcasting as a "somewhat nebulous and increasingly outdated theory".

Driving this attack politically was the continuing Conservative disquiet over the way broadcasters dealt with what Mrs Thatcher saw as the enemy. Even while Peacock was deliberating, a furious row had broken out between the BBC and Norman Tebbit over Kate Adie's reporting from Tripoli of the American bombing of Libya. On this front, the BBC defended itself stoutly, but a libel action brought by two right-wing MPs, Gerald Howarth and Neil Hamilton, over an edition of *Panorama* entitled *Maggie's Militant Tendency,* was settled on painfully expensive terms, above the heads of management, thanks to a U-turn by the Governors after the sudden death of the Chairman.

Soon afterwards, the Home Secretary who had appointed Peacock, Leon Brittan, had written to the BBC's Governors to urge they withdraw from the schedules a documentary entitled *Real Lives* that profiled a republican and a loyalist closely identified with the paramilitaries in Northern Ireland. The unprecedented decision by the Governors to view the programme before transmission, and delay its showing, eventually led to the peremptory dismissal of the BBC's Director-General, Alasdair Milne, by his new chairman, Marmaduke Hussey.

However, the Peacock Report gave the government no immediate purchase on the BBC. Indeed, all broadcasters had rallied round what was seen as a beleaguered Corporation, out of a mixture of narrow and broad self-interest. ITV and Channel 4 had even less desire to see the BBC funded by advertisements than the BBC itself; and all broadcasters found it opportune to endorse the collective virtues of a relatively closed and self-sustaining system. It was therefore all the more galling for the commercial broadcasters to find themselves fighting the post-Peacock battles on their own.

The BBC offered little support. Indeed, BBC Television's Director of Programmes, Michael Grade added fuel to the Peacock fire by suggesting that Channel 4's airtime should – as the Report had suggested – be sold separately from ITV's: a view he renounced when suddenly installed as Channel 4's new chief executive at a point in time when Channel 4's board was still hostile to the proposal. But within two years the board had concluded that this particular battle was not worth fighting. They gave higher priority to fending off the threat of direct political appointments to their own membership, and negotiating a safety net to smooth the now-accepted transition from dependence on ITV.

It was ITV that was most exposed by the Peacock process. In a remarkable development, the Monopolies and Mergers Commission was asked to investigate ITV's allegedly bloated labour costs. That the eventual findings were surprisingly positive was little consolation: Peacock had thoroughly entrenched in the Prime Minister's mind that ITV was – in her famous expression – "the last bastion" of restrictive practices. She used this phrase at a Downing Street seminar in 1987, at which the broadcast establishment had found themselves facing – amongst others – Thatcher, Lawson, Young, Peacock, the independent lobby and such Number 10 policy and industrial advisers as Brian Griffiths and Jeffrey Sterling.

Also there was Michael Green of Carlton Communications, a cousin by marriage of Lord Young and a contributor to Conservative funds, who had been frustrated in an attempted take-over of Thames Television by an IBA veto. His ambition to win an ITV licence for Carlton remained, and he was more than willing to use his political contacts eventually to achieve it.

The IBA was represented at the Downing Street seminar by its Director-General, John Whitney, who by his own admission put up a disastrous performance. ITV as a whole suffered a severe handbagging.

Mrs Thatcher had already decided to ride roughshod over the least palatable – to her taste – of Peacock's recommendations: progressive freedom of speech for broadcasters. Her 1987 election manifesto had included a promise to impose stricter control on portrayals of sex and violence. Within months of winning that election, the Conservatives established a Broadcasting Standards Council, appointing to its chairmanship Sir William Rees-Mogg, who had for long – from his vantage point as deputy chairman of its Governors – deplored the BBC's lack of editorial discipline. The BSC was given statutory status in the 1990 Broadcasting Act.

Meanwhile, in 1988, ITV broadcast an edition of *This Week* entitled *Death On The Rock*, analysing what had happened when three unarmed IRA terrorists had been shot dead on the streets of Gibraltar by an SAS squad. The Home Secretary, Douglas Hurd, who was responsible for broadcasting, declined a request from the Foreign Secretary, Sir Geoffrey Howe, to intervene with the IBA to prevent its transmission. So Howe took on the task himself. The IBA, having seen the film – which had been commissioned and vetted by me, as Director of Programmes at Thames – approved it for broadcast. Sir Geoffrey denounced both Thames and the IBA publicly. Most Fleet Street newspapers, taking their cue from Downing Street, were equally vituperative – expensively so for those which libelled one of the film's interviewees, Carmen Proetta. Mrs Thatcher was bitter: "worse than treason", she fulminated to a Japanese film crew.

That put an end to whatever doubts ITV might have had up to that point about the government's determination to impose the Peacock auction. The IBA, ever since Lord Thomson had replaced Lady Plowden at its head, had searched unsuccessfully for what he called "a better way" of allocating the ITV franchises than simply a beauty contest every ten or twelve years, when a handful of incumbents could expect to be dislodged for no better reason than "pour encourager les autres". After *Death On The Rock*, the IBA too came into the line of fire, along with its appointees, the ITV companies.

However, it would be wrong to see the auctioning of the ITV licences simply as a punitive measure. The idea of a spectrum market had a long and honourable pedigree, dating back till at least the 1950s. Harold Lever, one of Harold Wilson's brightest and most inventive cabinet ministers, had floated in the 1970's the idea of treating ITV franchises like North Sea oil fields – as scarce public assets whose return to the Treasury should be maximised. Even the Annan Report contained an appendix on "The Profits of Advertising-Financed Television", by a Dr Hindley, which asked why those who sought a right to broadcast did not "bid a price...in competition with other potential users".

In rejecting the idea, Annan had quoted approvingly Pilkington's view that there was "no natural connection between the best all-round qualification to provide a public service and the amount of money an applicant might offer or think it prudent to offer".

Peacock had no such resistance to economic logic, citing the New Zealand authorities who had described giving away spectrum as inherently inefficient and wasteful – like giving away wool. Only a spectrum market would allow Parliament and the regulators to place a proper value on the trade-off between the full commercial value of a broadcast licence and the reduction in that value flowing from the requirement to carry elements of public service programming within an otherwise commercial service. Whilst Peacock was sitting, the then leader of what were then the Social Democrats, David Owen, called for ITV licences to be auctioned.

In Peacock's view, a sensible balance could be achieved by setting a reserve price on each licence, laying down a threshold of quality any would-be bidder must cross, and then allowing the highest bidder to take the licence, thus maximising the returns to the Exchequer and squeezing waste out of the broadcast operation – equally desirable outcomes.

However, that there was a punitive element in the government's agenda was a conclusion hard to resist. What emerged in its 1988 White Paper – six months after the broadcast of *Death On The Rock* – was a version of ITV hard to recognise. ITV would not even be allowed to retain its name, instead being required to call itself channel three. The IBA, which had authorised *Death On The Rock*'s broadcast, was itself to be re-cast: as the Independent Television Commission. Independent Television News, the ITV news provider wholly owned by the contractors, would be required to bring in outside shareholders: this the result of private lobbying of Mrs Thatcher by a disgruntled news presenter using political connections to settle scores with owners insufficiently appreciative – so he thought – of ITN's potential.

In practice, these petty measures made little difference. ITV declined to change its name. The IBA did become the ITC, but with identical personnel – even absorbing the previously independent Cable Authority. The required change in ITN's ownership was largely ignored by the companies, using the simple device of placing their surplus shareholdings in ITN in deadlocked shell companies rather than in their broadcast arms.

But ITV lost on all the big issues. It was decided that the auction of licences would go ahead, without even the protection of the reserve price envisaged by Peacock. How the Treasury came to this bizarre arrangement – which defied common sense – has never been explained: it was certainly not for want of explanation to the Chancellor, Nigel Lawson. As a result, several successful bidders for ITV licences secured them at far below their market value, costing the Exchequer hundreds of millions of pounds over the years. As if to add insult to injury, the 1990 Broadcasting Act actually provided for subsequent renewal of the ITV licences to be based on a reserve market price set by the ITC – a belated application of rationality which could easily have been applied at the outset.

By the time the 1990 Act took final shape, Lawson had fallen out with Mrs Thatcher, and in the attendant cabinet re-shuffle, a former junior broadcasting minister, David Mellor, had been re-instated to make sense of the legislation. His first task had been to head off the possible resignation of the IBA chairman – who was also chairman-designate of the ITC – over the auction process. George Russell had made clear that he would not simply rubber-stamp the highest sealed bid. So Mellor tightened up the quality threshold and also conceded a right for the ITC to reject the highest bidder in exceptional circumstances.

Interestingly, Peacock himself went to see Mellor, to float the idea that there might be a trade-off between the level of bid and the quality of programming offered. However, as he told ITV's official history, "in the end this proposal was rejected – the government said 'no, there's a threshold: you get over Becher's Brook; it doesn't matter how high you jump, and then after that it's the bid'".

The exceptional circumstances clause proved to be something of a mirage. For instance, Thames Television, of which I was Programme Director at the time, had a formidable track record. But this was irrelevant in the licence auction, as complete newcomers to television broadcasting could apply, and therefore the only fair comparison would be between future promises, not past performance. Moreover, under new networking arrangements required by the ITC, individual licensees could not be held to account if their promised programmes were not later commissioned. With its high historic cost base – developed over three decades when a condition of holding a licence was the proven ability to deliver high-quality programmes – Thames felt it more than likely that it would be outbid by a competitor with no such historic cost base.

So it bid the most it felt it could afford for its own licence, and hoped that its clear edge in quality might trigger the exceptionality provision. This strategy failed, and it was galling to learn afterwards that George Russell felt Thames might have been better advised to bid less and thereby be able to promise even higher quality – the very trade-off proposed by Peacock and rejected by Mellor.

Of course, Thames was not the only casualty of the system. Some incumbents were rejected for over-bidding, even though they demonstrably possessed sufficient funds to afford their bid, or indeed had forecast future ITV revenue more accurately than the ITC. Another of those outbid – TV-AM – actually received a note of condolence from Mrs Thatcher herself, protesting "we didn't mean you": begging the obvious question of whom they did mean. Those of us at Thames were in little doubt.

Lawson later described the ITV auction as having had "an unusually high farce content". That so many of the franchises attracted only one or two bidders surely suggested a flaw in the design or the concept. Lawson, however, put the blame on the Home Office's last-minute meddling, echoing his former Prime Minister's sentiments, who felt that "unfortunately, in the Home Office, the broadcasters often found a ready advocate". Indeed, Mrs Thatcher attacked the results as "a compromise which turned out to be less satisfactory than when the ITC bestowed the franchises…in the old-fashioned way". By contrast, Mellor believed the Bill he had inherited to have been a "wretched" affair, reflecting the ideological preferences of ministers like Lawson who thought any "group of paint merchants could run a television company". But at least Michael Green finally achieved Carlton's desire to break into ITV.

ITV suffered another defeat, based on a calculated gamble. In an attempt to head off the separate selling of Channel 4's airtime, it espoused the idea of Channel 5 as a way of delivering – in due course – the competitive airtime market the advertisers so wanted. Interestingly, as late as 1984, Douglas Hurd, in his first stint as a Home Office minister, had told the House of Commons that it was "unlikely that a fifth channel could be added to those available from terrestrial transmitters". Not surprisingly, Peacock virtually ignored the prospect of a fifth channel, other than in the context of noting how the IBA's regulatory powers seemed to depend upon restricting entry of competitors into commercial television. The conflict between regulation and freedom of entry, said Peacock, "would become acute if there were a chance of a 5th or 6th channel for ordinary terrestrial broadcasting".

When the DTI and the BBC's engineers worked out in 1987 how to create a fifth network covering 65% of the country, ITV hoped its instant support for that channel to be advertising-supported would allow the more immediate danger of competition from Channel 4 to be averted. They pointed to Peacock's own statement that "even the direct sale of its own advertising by Channel 4 would breach the principle of no competition for the same source of revenue".

Peacock's rationale for splitting off Channel 4 was scarcely a principled one: he simply observed that "Channel Four is now at a point where its costs are of a similar order to the revenue from advertising". On that basis, he believed it should be offered the option of separation, despite his repeated assertion that once the protection of ITV from direct competition for revenue from rivals went, "the IBA will find it extremely difficult to enforce its standards".

The government's view of the issue ignored the potential impact on programme standards. The White Paper – whose subtitle, tellingly, was Competition, Choice and Quality, in that order – was brutally frank about whose interests should prevail. "Greater competition between those selling television air time – a pressing demand from those whose expenditure on advertising has paid for the independent television system – is essential. The government's wider proposals for a more competitive independent television sector mean that the place for Channel Four within such an integrated ITV system will no longer be available. Structural change is accordingly unavoidable". *Alice in Wonderland's* Queen of Hearts had found a kindred spirit.

When the Channel 4 board eventually took up the option, the ITV companies found they had lost on all fronts. They would face the licence auction, the separation of Channel 4 and competition from Channel 5, all virtually at the same time (though in practice, Channel 5 was delayed for four years after the first invitation to apply for the licence produced just one candidate, whose business plan the ITC rejected).

So Channel 5 – uniquely in the history of UK analogue terrestrial television – was triggered without the benefit of any committee of inquiry. Indeed, Sam Brittan protested at the very decision to allow it to be advertiser-funded: he thought it the ideal opportunity to test out subscription television, along the French lines of allocating a terrestrial frequency to Canal Plus, so greatly reducing the cost barriers to entry for the consumer.

This was not the only setback to Peacock's favoured project of subscription. Immediately after the Report was published, the Home Office commissioned a firm of consultants led by Charles Jonscher to advise on the feasibility of subscription. Jonscher's appointment can scarcely have disappointed Peacock. He had written a monograph in 1985 that might have served as a blueprint for the Peacock proposals. He had seen the future – the addressable set-top converter – and thought it not only worked, but provided "the essential basis for an efficient market to exist". At the right price, "it would be possible to introduce such devices into all UK television sets, and then to scramble the transmissions of the BBC and any other non-advertiser-supported services in order to introduce the new transaction system".

Jonscher had few doubts. "At some time in the future, perhaps five years from now, the price of these devices will have fallen to the point where the BBC could scramble its services without presenting the poorer members of the community with an excessive cost barrier if they are to continue obtaining BBC services. The licence fee could then become conditional on the viewer's wish to view BBC programmes".

Jonscher pointed to the fact that the high cost of VCRs and rented tapes "has not deterred a very large proportion of UK households from subscribing to this new medium", as he called it. "This can make us confident that television channels...will be able to command substantial revenues if financed on a subscription basis. For this reason the BBC need not be afraid of switching to this new technology at such time when the price drops to a sufficiently low level – perhaps in the region of £50 per unit. This, and not commercial advertising, is clearly the correct long run solution to the funding problem".

Jonscher's report, published in 1987, was the same length as Peacock's and was similarly laden with graphs and tables. But his conclusions were utterly at variance with Peacock's, and indeed with his own previously published views. Sophisticated analyses had led him to the clear conclusion that subscription was inferior to both the licence fee and advertising as a means of funding broadcast services, in terms of consumer welfare. Moreover, he calculated, neither BBC1 nor BBC2 could be expected to sustain themselves simply through subscription.

In addition to these "negative economic impacts of transferring BBC financing substantially to subscription basis", Jonscher was in no doubt that "in a subscription environment...the BBC would... change its programme mix substantially...if subscription were to be the only source of BBC income...the Corporation would have to switch almost completely from the current mix to one which relies heavily on 'premium' programming" – by which he meant sport and movies.

This was a blow for the subscription lobby. Unhappily for them, the mass of detail in the Jonscher Report effectively concealed its profound methodological weakness. The reason Jonscher emphasised sport and movies in his analysis was that the only successful pay services available to him for examination depended on these genres. There was no precedent for a generalist service, let alone one with a pre-existing 50% share of viewing, transferring to subscription. Indeed, Jonscher could not even imagine more than three pay services flourishing in any market. His analysis therefore failed to address the BBC's unique position.

More importantly, his entire edifice of consumer welfare calculations was built on the flimsy base of interviews with just 84 participants in 13 discussion groups, who were, as Jonscher himself conceded, highly unrepresentative of the population as a whole in their viewing habits. Despite the report stating that "the purpose of this survey was not to generate statistically valid quantitative results", all the Report's findings on consumer behaviour and welfare were calculated from the responses of these 84, even though when asked such a basic matter as how many hours a week they might purchase from the four channels, "more than a third of the respondents found this question too difficult to answer".

To compound this gross error, Jonscher then constructed all his calculations on the assumption of one television set per home. As Peacock had already made clear, however, a key attraction of subscription was the opportunity it represented to restore buoyancy and fairness to the funding of the BBC by making a charge per set rather than a charge per home. Only after having arrived at his negative findings did Jonscher lamely add: "we note in conclusion one potential attraction of the use of access control technology for the collection of the licence fee, namely the ability to charge a separate licence fee for each set in the home". Given that the average number of sets per home was already nearly two, the failure to accommodate this factor in his calculations effectively rendered the Jonscher Report worthless as a document to shape policy, despite the wealth of information it had assembled.

Nonetheless, the Jonscher findings became the common wisdom, and a range of witnesses, including the BBC, the IBA, the Home Office and the Broadcasting Research Unit, cited them to the House of Commons Home Affairs Committee, which held extensive hearings in 1988 into the future of broadcasting. Only two academic economists from the London Business School – who happened strongly to support the licence fee – challenged Jonscher's findings on subscription, believing the likelihood to be very small indeed of people opting out of the BBC if the charge for it became voluntary.

Indeed, the LBS then embarked upon a two-year research project, jointly led by a former senior research specialist from the BBC. Their report on "Viewers' Willingness to Pay" was published in 1990. Its ingenious methodology demonstrated that "British television viewers are willing to pay far higher prices than the current licence fee to keep their mainstream channels...the results suggest that BBC-TV could easily be financed by subscription instead of the licence fee: if the BBC were to charge as much as the market would bear, it could be highly profitable". The LBS still preferred licence-fee funding, on the grounds that subscription operating costs appeared at the time to be greater than the cost of licence fee evasion and collection. However, even the LBS failed to build into its study the multi-set factor, resting its case simply on the finding that "almost no-one would stop watching BBC1 or (mostly) BBC2 with voluntary subscriptions at about the licence fee overall level".

The Home Affairs Committee had published its report in the summer of 1988. It broadly endorsed Peacock's approach, with the addition of the early introduction of Channel Five and of a five-year timetable for a 25% independent production quota, ahead of Peacock's ten-year target of 40%. Despite the fact that most of the independent producers were to the left politically, the Conservatives warmed to them as mini-capitalists who would be a force for greater efficiency in broadcasting. In my days as an independent, I had once led deputations to Alasdair Milne at the

BBC and Lady Plowden at the IBA, asking for a 2% quota. Now the government bludgeoned a 25% voluntary quota into existence, with the threat of a higher statutory figure if the BBC and ITV failed to comply.

So what had been almost an afterthought in the Peacock Report was swiftly implemented, and was to lead to profound change in the industry. The partial disaggregation of what had previously been a locked vertical structure of resources, production, broadcasting, transmission and distribution set loose a remorseless logic, not least in the BBC. Its effects are still being felt.

The Home Affairs Committee also reminded the Government of Peacock's desire for peritelevision sockets to become mandatory in new television sets from 1988. It now recommended shifting the date to 1990 to reflect the intervening delay. However, the Jonscher Report had largely undermined this notion, pointing out that there were many means of achieving the same outcome, and arguing that the issue of such sockets really lay outside its terms of reference. So it had made no recommendation.

Curiously, the Home Office itself, in evidence to the Commons Committee, claimed Jonscher had recommended against the mandatory socket. In any event, the 1988 White Paper remained unconvinced, whilst still arguing that the BBC must prepare for the eventual introduction of subscription in place of the licence fee. "To provide a financial incentive" for such a transfer, "the Government intends after April 1991 to agree licence fee increases of less than the RPI increase".

The peritelevision socket – or the scart connection as it later became known – eventually became mandatory for larger television sets through a European Commission directive. But by then, the whole issue of subscription had been hi-jacked by Rupert Murdoch, who proved in spectacular fashion what the research from the National Consumer Council and the London Business School had suggested – that the dissatisfaction with the existing four channels expressed by nearly half of all viewers, and the willingness of viewers to pay for television far beyond the level of the licence fee, could be converted into a substantial revenue stream.

By an odd coincidence, the day the Broadcasting Act of 1990 had received the Royal Assent was also the day that Murdoch's Sky Television had merged with its IBA-sponsored rival, British Satellite Broadcasting, in the form of BSkyB. This deal had outraged a helpless IBA, as well as the liberal press, especially when they discovered that Murdoch had forewarned Mrs Thatcher of it at a private meeting. Indeed, nearly all the sins attributed to Murdoch in the satellite television business are also blamed on Thatcher, who is assumed to have helped her political admirer and fellow outsider in his broadcasting successes.

The facts do little to support this conspiracy hypothesis. Murdoch had rescued London Weekend Television soon after its 1968 launch, when it fell into financial and managerial crisis. But the regulator at the time – the ITA – had baulked at letting such a commercially-minded Australian entrepreneur actually take over the running of LWT. He had bowed out, amid much bitterness, and concentrated on building up his newspaper empire – and here there is no question but that the Thatcher cabinet facilitated his take-over of Times Newspapers by not referring it for a monopolies inquiry.

In television, however, Murdoch was spinning his wheels. It was Robert Maxwell who was the potential beneficiary of the Government's mid-1980's de-regulation of cable. (Not that Maxwell had the business skills to capitalise on this, even letting a half share in the hugely valuable MTV Europe slip through his fingers.) Murdoch, meanwhile, was distributing his Sky satellite channel to European cable systems, losing tens of millions over six years before accepting that there was virtually no pan-European advertising market. When the rules were changed in 1985 to allow domestic premises to install dishes, it was to facilitate the success of UK DBS, not Rupert Murdoch.

Meanwhile, initiatives at both the European Union and the Council of Europe (which embraced 21 countries rather than the EU's then 12) led to agreements requiring all member states to accept satellite transmissions emanating from other member states. Some degree of harmonised regulation was established, with the UK supporting Swedish moves to make such regulation realistic. Murdoch played no part in this ground-clearing process, but was swift to respond when one EU member, Luxembourg, defied the working agreement amongst European telephone companies – nearly all state-owned monopolies – that medium-powered satellites should only be used for telecommunications purposes.

A Luxembourg company, SES/Astra, wanted to use one of Luxembourg's internationally agreed space slots for a satellite targeting 60 centimetre dishes that could be attached to domestic premises across virtually the whole of Western Europe. There was much regulatory disapproval – when Thames chose to invest in Astra, the IBA queried the satellite's legal status, echoing the allegations of piracy aimed at Radio Luxembourg in the 1930's. But when BT broke ranks with its fellow telephone companies and chose to support Astra, official hostility fell away. Murdoch promptly booked four transponders on the satellite to re-launch Sky Television as Sky One, along with news, film and sports channels.

His surprise move took off guard the BSB consortium that had won the right to use the official high-powered UK satellite slots, beating off other applicants that had included Michael Green and Rupert Murdoch. BSB dismissed the Sky threat, mistakenly believing the Astra dishes would retail at two or three times the price of their own smaller ones. Launching 14 months later, BSB could never erode Sky's head-start. Both operators lost huge amounts of money, with Murdoch's entire business – News Corporation – coming close to financial meltdown. In the end, it was BSB's shareholders who finally lost their nerve, conceding management control to Murdoch of the merged company, despite the equal split of ownership.

Thatcher's role in all this was never more than marginal. She could no more have prevented Sky's launch than the eventual merger. That BSB was burdened with unnecessary costs and regulations simply reflected a long history of governments believing they could indulge their prejudices irrespective of market forces. It is true that Sky was boosted heavily by the Murdoch press – but no more so than ONDigital being boosted by ITV. Indeed, if any Conservative-supporting media operator can be said to have benefited in business terms from government decisions, Michael Green's is the name that springs to mind.

In any case, what made Sky work was not so much the merger – in December 1990, BSkyB was still losing £10 million a week – as determined management, a close understanding of consumer preferences and technological innovation. Here, too, Murdoch was to be accused of unfair practices, in building a vertically-integrated company that owned subscriber management systems, encryption technology, a smart card company, a dish installation business, transponder leases, production and transmission facilities, and access to the films and series produced by the News Corporation subsidiary, Fox.

Yet the truth is that, without all those aspects to its business, BSkyB would not have been a business – and nobody was going to do it for Murdoch. Indeed, most competitors forecast he would fail – because old-fashioned PAL signals could not be encrypted, or the smart cards would be swamped by pirate versions, or people would refuse to have unsightly dishes on their walls, or British broadcasting was simply too good for anything other than premium movies or sport to find a market. That premium movies and sport only take a quarter of satellite and cable viewing today, and that dozens of niche and general channels have managed to flourish off the back of Murdoch's enormous gamble and investment, simply demonstrates the weakness of conventional thinking over many years.

But the terrestrial broadcasters fought back, finding a strong ally in the cable industry that the BBC had denounced to the Hunt Inquiry as socially divisive. The cable programme offering was immeasurably strengthened by the availability of Sky programming, but cable's marginal costs were largely in Sky's control and marginal revenue largely flowed to Sky's pockets. The plaintive cries from the cable companies led to regular OFT investigations of Sky's alleged abuse of its dominant position. No complaint was ever upheld, but the clear public perception was created that Sky was an unscrupulous competitor.

ITV suffered a major psychological blow when it lost its biggest sporting contract – top level league football – to Sky in 1992. But its revenues were barely affected, and the importance of the Premier League to Sky has been much exaggerated: the biggest single boost to Sky's business came, not from the launch of the Premier League in August 1992, but from the launch of the Multi-Channels package in September 1993. The proportion of sport on Sky that has been diverted from terrestrial television – the biggest fear of successive committees of inquiry in relation to pay television – is less than 5%. The BBC has lost more major sport to ITV, Channel 4 and even Channel 5 than to Sky.

Even so, a substantial body of anti-Murdoch opinion, carefully guided by the BBC, managed in 1996 to overturn the government majority in the House of Lords, and secure a ban on the listed sporting events – eight in all, including the Cup Final and Wimbledon – being sold exclusively to limited circulation channels. The BBC had also judged it worthwhile to invest in expert evidence to support cable complaints against Sky. And it strongly supported moves within the European Parliament to impose tight controls on the development of the next generation of pay television, using digital technology.

To be fair, the BBC could properly claim to be seeking to defend the public interest as well as its own interest in all this – and for the BBC, the stakes were high: digital could make or break the Corporation. For all players, the attractions of digital were considerable. The new technology increased the number of channels that could be squeezed into any distribution pipeline, promised improved picture and sound quality, and permitted greater interactivity, particularly as television, telephones and computers could all now use the same language. Those who had complained – rightly or wrongly – of Sky's alleged abuse of its dominant position in analogue pay television were determined that, if it achieved a similar position in digital, it would be unable to abuse it.

Even the Conservatives – even under Thatcher – introduced media cross-ownership rules, designed to prevent the biggest newspaper proprietors from owning more than a small stake in terrestrial television. Murdoch's critics felt this missed the point: it was in satellite pay television that he had been allowed to build an immensely powerful position. Yet who could have prevented it? Satellite transponders were not a scarce resource – the IBA currently licenses over 200 satellite services. Moreover, if they were leased from a non-UK source, they were not in the government's gift either to allocate or to regulate in great detail. Any attempt to impose tight ownership rules on non-domestic satellite channels would have been self-defeating: operations would simply have transferred, perfectly legally, elsewhere in the EU, costing thousands of jobs in the UK.

Instead, a new form of regulation emerged, based on fair trading rather than service content. The competition authorities required Sky to make all its programming available to its cable rivals, though conversely cable-exclusive programming could be withheld from the satellite platform. Sky's rate-card for its services was regulated. It was forbidden from requiring cable companies to take one of its channels as a condition of acquiring any other of them. And however far ahead Sky had travelled in analogue, in digital it would have to start again.

In digital, the forces wary of Sky identified two areas where new controls might be imposed. The first battle was over the design of decoder boxes themselves, which took place at the industrial, regulatory and political levels in Europe. A determined attempt – with the BBC and British MEPs very much to the fore – was made to impose either a ban on proprietary conditional access systems in digital boxes, or a separate common interface that could be used by broadcasters free-riding on the back of the pioneer investors after a sufficient population of boxes had been established. In the end, industrial logic prevailed over political preference: neither measure was implemented, and the prospect of digital dying for lack of investors faded. However, Sky and other users of proprietary systems were faced with an array of regulatory controls against abuse.

The other battlefield concerned the electronic programme guide – the navigation system that enabled viewers to steer through the plethora of choice available in digital. The possibility of manipulation was clear. The BBC even produced a £10,000 cod video showing how a purported Sky EPG might banish BBC services to remote parts of the system. This backfired somewhat when Sky was able to demonstrate how the BBC's own listings guides – on television and in print – discriminated against its competitors, especially non-terrestrial ones. However, the investment paid off, as ministers and regulators were persuaded to impose strict conditions on the way EPGs were designed.

In the event, as the experience of Sky Multi-Channels had already shown, far from wanting to exclude rivals from its platform, Sky was keen for all of them to come on board, with prominent slots on the EPG. It was Sky's competitors who chose to withhold their services – notably, ITV and ITV2; and that was because their owners now had their own platform they wished to favour, as a result of the biggest single development in the politics of digital: digital terrestrial television, or DTT.

In preparing for the digital age, the BBC's most important victory was in persuading Whitehall and the other terrestrial broadcasters of the virtues of DTT. That the existing analogue masts could be used for DTT was easy enough to see. That up to thirty channels could be squeezed into a terrestrial system which currently barely provided five was also evident. That most people would be able to receive these without a dish or cable box, but on their existing aerial, seemed likely.

For cable and satellite, the transfer to digital was a business decision, not a political one. What was harder to understand was either who would pay for DTT transmission, costing at least £70 million a year in addition to the costs of the analogue terrestrial system, or which consumers would be attracted to such a limited array of channels – fewer even than in analogue cable and satellite, and a fraction of what these platforms could offer in digital. Yet there were powerful political and regulatory attractions in DTT.

For Westminster politicians, in the absence of DTT, there was the unwelcome prospect of a digital television system effectively outside their control and potentially dominated by Murdoch. And paradoxically, a limited capacity system, allocated by UK regulators, held out the possibility of preserving a central place for the traditional broadcasters, even in the age of spectrum plenty. The dizzy visions of electronic publishing, beyond the effective reach of any regulators, could be blinkered off in a reinvented version of spectrum scarcity.

A typical trade-off was arranged. In return for all the terrestrial broadcasters agreeing to transmit their analogue services in parallel in digital for many years, they were all allocated additional capacity in the best half of the thirty-channel DTT system. This they could use to start launching new services within a controlled environment that they could continue to dominate.

All the terrestrial broadcasters received financial favours from the government sufficient to induce their co-operation – in effect, the public is paying for the DTT transmission system. The other half of the capacity was put out to tender to commercial operators.

The winning bid came from a consortium of Carlton and Granada – who now owned two-thirds of ITV – and BSkyB itself. However, under pressure from the European competition authorities, and the telecommunications regulator OFTEL, the ITC forced BSkyB to withdraw as a shareholder, but to leave its promised programme services in place. The government, through the ITC, also created a complex set of ownership and content rules for DTT. Undeterred by the experience of the 1980s, and without the benefit of any public inquiry on the post-war pattern, a politically-driven broadcasting agenda had been re-instated, just at a time when the Peacock era of direct consumer choice appeared within reach.

It has been a surprising turn of events, not without risk. Both Conservative and Labour administrations have seen the virtue of a limited attempt at shaping the digital market. The public justification has been that the consumer benefits of digital broadcasting are potentially very large, and that a three-platform system should hasten its rapid adoption. DTT also allowed consumers to switch to digital simply by purchasing a digital television set, without any need to subscribe to pay channels or purchase a separate decoder. Moreover, the faster the universal take-up of digital, the more quickly the government could re-possess the analogue terrestrial spectrum, so delivering a potential one-off windfall in the multi-billion pound sale of that spectrum for telecommunications use.

The reality of that windfall should not be taken for granted. The ITC has already warned that switching off the analogue broadcast system is likely to take even longer than the 21 years that passed between deciding to switch off the 405-line transmitters in favour of 625-line ones, and actually doing it in 1985. Today, television sets last much longer, each home has on average nearly three sets, and nearly every home has a video recorder. Virtually every single piece of functioning hardware will need to be upgraded to digital before switching off analogue becomes politically possible. The idea that a switch-off date even five years ahead could be announced, say when 75% of homes have one digital set, is fraught with danger.

The politics of digital are far more complex than the version of broadcasting Peacock imagined. Economic regulation has emerged as a key factor in government involvement. Ministers are now contemplating how to manage the mix of content and competition regulation, as broadcasting converges with other digital technologies.

The broadcasting market has grown rapidly, but there is still a major degree of public sector provision – not just through the licence fee and the cost of Welsh and Gaelic services, but in the implicit public subsidy of Channels 3, 4 and 5, who pay reduced – or nil – amounts to gain access to their valuable frequencies, in exchange for accepting public service obligations. Even in the age of ostensible spectrum plenty, there is still a premium for scarce terrestrial frequencies, on which the great majority of homes are dependent.

The fair competition issues now go well beyond Sky's activities. We have already seen the ITC issue a new set of cross-promotion guidelines after ITV was adjudged to have abused the right to promote digital television in promotional airtime by supporting the terrestrial platform in opposition to satellite. New questions come thick and fast.

Should ITV and its effective subsidiary, ONDigital, be allowed to bid jointly for major sports rights, such as the Champions League football, when no other broadcaster has similar access to both free-to-air and pay channels? Should free-to-air rights and pay rights for such championships be separated and sold as stand-alone packages, as is required for live and highlights rights by the ITC's rules on listed events? Is it unfair to advertisers when their costs are driven up several percentage points by Carlton and Granada selling £50 million of their own airtime to their own group companies? Should the BBC be allowed to buy all rights to a tennis tournament, knowing full well that it will schedule only the highlights of the final on its main services, relegating live coverage to BBC Choice, available to just a small minority of homes?

How substantial a player in the commercial market-place do we want the BBC to become? Are its commercial activities abroad as sensitive as those at home? Does it matter if its commercial arm – which makes its money out of the exploitation of licence-funded programmes – loses money on investments overseas? How does the BBC balance the short-term maximisation of revenue from licence-funded programming with the opportunity to build capital assets using that material as collateral? Is it right to require licence-fee payers to pay again to see programming they have funded, when opportunities arise for that material to be sold to free-to-air broadcasters?

To what extent should the BBC involve itself in the new pay television and digital market? When Channel 4 launched its premium film service, Film 4, it put £30 million at risk. Given that Channel 4 pays nothing for its highly valuable broadcast frequencies, that investment might be considered to be public money diverted from the programme budget. If the BBC used the licence fee for such a service – whether or not it proved profitable – there would be loud protests. The BBC promised Peacock that, after the failure of its DBS ambitions, it would not venture into the pay television business again. Instead, it puts non-cash assets into commercial partnerships with the likes of Flextech and Discovery, and uses licence fee cash to fund new free-to-air services.

Even these free-to-air services, however, create controversy. Sky has complained to the European Commission that its Sky News service was damaged when the BBC made available to cable companies at no charge its own licence-funded News 24. All the BBC's free-to-air digital services constitute in effect a transfer of resources away from those services available to 99% of households and 100% of licence fee payers, to those homes who have invested in multi-channel technology.

This conundrum goes to the heart of the BBC funding review, chaired by Goldman Sachs chief international economist Gavyn Davies, appropriately just fifty years after Lord Beveridge was announced as chairman of the first of the post-war committees of inquiry. The Davies review is not a full inquiry – but its terms cover much the same ground as Peacock's, though with an emphasis on fair trading and how to supplement the licence fee rather than on advertising and sponsorship specifically.

Peacock felt entitled to draw his inquiry much wider than just how to fund the BBC, because of the way other media were drawn into the argument. The likelihood is that Davies will quickly reject advertising and sponsorship as meaningful sources of BBC revenue, just as Peacock did. He will also find the BBC's potential for generating commercial revenue limited in scope, as well as hedged with competition issues. All the signs are that, like Peacock, he will assume that there is no realistic political option for indexing the licence fee ahead of inflation, and that some other source of restoring the BBC's revenue buoyancy and funding its legitimate digital ambitions will need to be found.

A clear temptation is a digital supplement to the licence fee, just as happened when television and then colour were introduced. Those who used the new services paid for them. At a stroke, commercial and political objections to the BBC's digital channels would fall by the wayside. Moreover, because every digital decoder would have an automatic switch to prevent access by non-payers of the digital supplement, and every digital television sale could be recorded centrally, the digital licence would be easier to collect than the analogue one, and multi-set homes would, equitably, pay proportionately more. Peacock's famous stage two – the subscription era – would be accomplished by the transfer to digital.

For the digital pioneers – broadcasters, manufacturers, retailers – it would be a heavy temporary blow, a potential brake on a politically desirable technology switch, made worse by being introduced only months after they had laid their digital bets. Yet it would restore the principle laid down by Beveridge, Pilkington, Annan and Peacock that the different BBC services should be funded by their users.

Is it necessary? Perhaps not in the short term. The funding gap between the BBC and ITV has proved as illusory as Kennedy's missile gap. Peacock and Jonscher imagined it might reach £1 billion a year by the end of the century – but it has not materialised, even a dozen years later. The BBC has squeezed hundreds of millions from its costs, thanks to internal reforms accelerated by the introduction of independents. It has kept over £200 million from the sale of its transmitters – a rare concession from a post-Thatcher Conservative administration. It has secured special increases in the licence fee to fund its initial steps in digital. Meanwhile, ITV and Channel 4, though prospering, have seen their revenue and programme budgets staying only just ahead of the BBC's. Against the expectations of many, the BBC and its licence fee are secure until at least 2006. The BBC, putting its Peacock evidence behind it, has hardened its support for the licence fee. Subscription funding may still beckon, but only distantly.

The BBC's central role in British broadcasting has remained a constant through the succession of post-war inquiries. So has the desire to regulate broadcasting through its incremental points of growth. From the start of the 1980s, the consumer came to displace the broadcaster as the key figure in shaping government policy: but the instinct for monopoly, the habit of managing the market and the belief that the man in Whitehall knows best die hard in political circles. Consumers must seemingly be protected not only from commercial predators but also from themselves. The digital age whose joyous freedoms Peter Jay delineated 30 years ago may soon be with us: but it has paradoxically begun with a renewed impetus for regulation, not just in the UK, but in the EU generally.

If there is a lesson from the last fifty years, it is that broadcasting continues to defy the normal rules of consumer provision. As Pilkington put it, controls that derived from technical reasons have assumed a cultural, social and political dimension. The politics of digital are in many ways the politics of analogue writ large. Perhaps the time will soon come for another full-scale inquiry, to unravel the many policy threads that digital broadcasting entwines. And perhaps the ensuing report will permit a postscript to this series of lectures.

[7]
Davies and the Digital Licence Fee

25 November 1999

Between the publication of the Peacock Report and that of the Davies Report, thirteen years elapsed. Have Governments been remiss in leaving the structure of broadcasting unexamined through a period of profound change? Perhaps yes, if we look at the unprecedented transformation of the entire industry in that period. Or perhaps no, in that if we exclude the narrow-remit Hunt Report, thirteen years turns out to be the average gap between major investigations into broadcasting in general and the BBC in particular – Beveridge in 1949, Pilkington in 1962, Annan in 1977, Peacock in 1986 and Davies in 1999.

Of course, that already begs the question as to whether the Davies Report is on a par with the other four. The Davies Panel, by its very nomenclature, seemed subtly down-graded from the Committee status of the other Reports. And it was allowed only six months to complete its work: no more than the three-man Hunt Committee, and only half the time allocated to Peacock. Moreover, as the Panel's Report was at pains to point out, its brief and its timetable precluded any investigation of the broadcasting industry as a whole, or even the nature and purpose of public service broadcasting. Indeed, even the BBC's status and rationale were beyond the Panel's remit.

The same was true of the licence fee. When the terms of what was described as a "BBC Funding Review" were announced in October 1998, it was made clear that those charged with the task must "start from the position that the licence fee is sustainable at least until the review of the Charter due in the run-up to 2006".

That the licence fee would persist as the BBC's main source of funding for twenty years after publication of his own Report would have surprised Peacock. That it did so was largely the result of Mrs Thatcher bringing her guns to bear on commercial television rather than the BBC, and then losing office in 1990. Her successor, John Major, displayed far less hostility to the BBC. He hived off broadcasting from the Home Office, and created a Department of National Heritage, whose first Secretary of State was none other than the salvage merchant of the 1990 Broadcasting Act, David Mellor.

By this time, the BBC had acquired a Director-General, John Birt, determined to make the Corporation more palatable to the Conservatives, editorially, structurally and financially. Despite (or perhaps because of) a rapid turnover of ministers at the DNH – four in six years – Birt and his corporate strategists were able to secure a ten-year renewal of the BBC Charter and a five-year licence fee settlement designed to carry the BBC into the digital era.

Tony Blair's electoral victory in May 1997 saw the DNH turned into the DCMS – the Department for Culture, Media and Sport. A former shadow DNH spokesman, Chris Smith, was appointed Secretary of State. His survival through two cabinet re-shuffles means that he will be the only post-war minister to have both introduced a major broadcasting inquiry and decided whether to implement its findings.

It was Chris Smith who laid down the remit of the "BBC Funding Review", as he termed it – how to supplement the licence fee so as to enhance "the BBC's position as the nation's foremost public service broadcaster", whilst keeping a balance between the BBC's public service and commercial activities. A specific additional task was to examine the concessionary licence fee scheme.

By the end of November, he had found his chairman, the prominent economist and long-term Labour Party advisor, Gavyn Davies. By January, eight formidable panellists had been named, suitably balanced between the sexes and the parties; though one of the eight was promptly promoted to the BBC's Board of Governors. Nine weeks were allowed for evidence to be submitted, with the final Report appearing four months later.

If that seemed a tight timetable for such a major issue, suspicion that the Panel's conclusions were anyway foregone was inevitably aroused by the identity of the chairman. Gavyn Davies, after all, was famous for many reasons – his support of Southampton Football Club, his immense wealth as a partner in Goldman Sachs, and his closeness to the Labour Party hierarchy, underlined by his wife's role in the private office of the Chancellor of the Exchequer – he actually met her whilst working in Downing Street for the previous Labour administration.

He is also indelibly connected with the digital licence fee: a notion he had discussed in an influential pamphlet funded by the BBC and published in 1997. Davies had co-authored "Broadcasting, Society and Policy in the Multimedia Age" with his old Oxford tutor and fellow Labour Party economic advisor, Andrew Graham. The chapters are not individually attributed, but it was no secret that Graham wrote most of the philosophical section and Davies the financial portion.

The pamphlet urged that the BBC be funded at a level that kept pace with the commercial sector. This argument was popular within the BBC and would be cited in the Davies Report as forming part of the Director-General's grand vision for the BBC in the New Statesman lecture that John (now Sir John) Birt gave in July 1999:

> Unless and until the BBC's income grows as the nation's income grows, and as the broadcasting industry's income grows, the BBC will gradually, slowly, imperceptibly, incrementally diminish in relation to the rest of broadcasting and will play a reducing part in this nation's life.

This bid, not just to inflation-proof the BBC's income, but to link it to GDP and/or broadcasting industry revenue, was indicative of the scale of the BBC's financial ambitions. Irrespective of how good or cost-effective or necessary the BBC's current level of service might be, it should automatically be granted yet more access to public funds generated by the most socially regressive of tax mechanisms, simply to preserve an arithmetical relationship between its income and some more or less relevant measure.

As far as broadcasting industry revenues are concerned, the evidence adduced by Davies was that the BBC's income has actually kept abreast of or ahead of revenues for its two main television rivals, ITV and Channel 4. It is true there has been a surge of subscription payments, but the broadcasters who receive these are only marginally competitive with the BBC. Their focus is very much on thematic and niche channels – many of which constitute a revenue source, rather than drain, for the BBC, in buying from its library. As for the subscription sports and movie channels, these are overwhelmingly purchase rights that are either not available to free-to-air stations, or are beyond their collective financial reach. To argue from BSkyB's success to raising the licence fee pro rata is profoundly misleading.

Like so many economists who were subsequently persuaded by the BBC to write similar essays on broadcasting policy, despite lacking specific expertise in broadcasting, Graham and Davies took for granted that the BBC was a good thing, that it faced growing competition, and that therefore it needed extra funding.

With the same kind of abstract arguments, the licence fee was accepted as the method of funding the BBC that was fairest or most effective or most conducive to quality broadcasting. The implicit logic of such a position was that in order to sustain an arbitrary proportion of audience share below which the BBC could not be allowed to drop for fear that the licence fee might become unsustainable, the level of the licence fee would keep having to be raised in the face of the rapid growth in choice available to the viewer. The less you watched the BBC, the more you would have to pay for it until the sheer weight of its spending power commanded your viewing attention.

The merits or demerits of these arguments need not detain us here: suffice it to say that the Davies essay, in acknowledging the apparent need to increase the BBC's income ahead of inflation, and the political difficulty of doing so simply by raising the licence fee, suggested either that multi-set households should pay extra or that owners of digital televisions should be charged a supplementary fee.

The multi-set concept, of course, is close to the subscription model preferred by Peacock, with homes deriving most benefit from the BBC's services paying proportionately more. This is already standard in cable and satellite homes, where the facility to allow subscription services to be chosen on more than one TV set in the household costs an additional fee. However, in non-subscription homes, collecting multiple licence fees presented such severe practical problems that the Davies Panel eventually discarded the idea.

In his 1997 pamphlet, Davies seemed anyway more taken by the digital licence fee, comparing it with the introduction of an extra licence fee for television (over and above radio) and for colour (over and above black-and-white television) when the BBC had made previous step shifts in its provision of services. He recognised difficulties with the proposal: the pace of introduction of digital was hard to predict accurately, so creating uncertainty for the BBC; a disincentive to digital take-up might frustrate government initiatives, such as the spread of the "information society"; and if analogue switch-off forced households into involuntary higher digital costs, the whole concept might become unacceptably unpopular.

At this stage, it is important to note that Davies made no link between the BBC's provision of additional digital services and the digital licence fee: it was the price of gaining access to the benefits of digital, by whomsoever provided, and was designed simply to restore buoyancy to BBC revenues to be spent on protecting market share. If Davies was aware of the principle of separate funding for separate services enunciated by the Beveridge, Pilkington and Annan Committees, he betrayed no knowledge of it here.

Also at this stage, Davies imagined such increased buoyancy in BBC revenues to be a continuing process, with a levy of £45 per digital home bringing in nearly £150 million extra each year by 2005 (a figure remarkably similar to his Report's eventual recommendation) rising to £970 million per annum a decade later (more in line with the BBC's now declared ambitions).

It would be wrong, as a matter of record, to attribute solely to Gavyn Davies the notion of a digital licence fee. Indeed, after publication of the Davies Report, at least one newspaper claimed that it was Gordon Brown's idea, from before his becoming Chancellor, and that Gavyn Davies in his 1997 pamphlet was simply the mouthpiece being operated by the puppet master (in *The Sun*'s less than elegant phrase).

Be that as it may, the idea certainly had earlier provenance. In December 1996, when John Birt and his chairman, Sir Christopher Bland, were giving evidence to the Commons National Heritage Committee, Labour MP and licence fee critic Joe Ashton asked whether the BBC intended to have a digital licence fee, following the precedent of the colour licence fee. Birt's answer would be quoted ad nauseum by opponents of the digital licence fee during and after the Davies Panel's deliberations.

> Neither the Government nor we are inclined in that direction, I suppose for two main reasons. The first is that a higher licence fee for receiving digital programmes would in effect be a tax on innovation and might hold up the development of digital delivery systems. The second point is that colour was quite unusual in being a technical innovation to be funded in that way. Other innovations like FM for instance have been funded simply by the increases in the basic licence fee.

The second "reason" offered by Birt actually confused two issues. There is a difference between paying for new services only receivable by adopting a new technology – such as colour TV – and funding new delivery systems for existing services – which are nearly always justifiable out of the basic licence fee, in that you are entitled to those services whatever the cost of delivering them to you. On the same principle, Scots pay no higher a licence fee than Londoners despite the far greater cost of transmitting the BBC's services to them.

It was the first reason proffered by Birt that was clearly the important one, and it was amplified by his Deputy Director-General, Bob Phillis, at the same Commons Committee session. A digital licence fee would "inhibit and delay the growth of digital broadcasting in Britain and it would certainly push back that time where a government of the future might be able to consider closing down the analogue broadcasting systems in Britain".

This was not an impromptu response to verbal questions. Six months later, in June 1997, the BBC published the outcome of a public consultation on its planned digital services. "We do not agree," said the BBC, "that a differential licence fee for those who make use of the public digital services would be practical or desirable. A premium on the licence fee might discourage the take-up of digital public services. In any case, viewers opting for the new services will have to pay extra for the necessary equipment".

Clearly, the BBC had not anticipated that competition in the market place might reduce or even eliminate equipment costs for new digital households. In any event, another part of the document revealed that the BBC was perfectly content to fund new digital services out of the basic licence fee. "The cost of the BBC's new digital services", it said, "will represent only a small proportion of the BBC's total expenditure. We estimate that, after five years" – i.e., by June 2002 – "annual spending on digital services will be equivalent to 9% of funds from the licence fee".

In fact, the BBC has already exceeded that 9% level. And digital programme services, of course, are a separate category of costs from investment in digital transmission, which few would deny to be a legitimate charge to the licence fee. Unfortunately, a degree of ambiguity had been left by the 5-year licence settlement negotiated during the last months of the Conservative government. This had been, in economic parlance, front-end-loaded, allowing the BBC licence fee increases ahead of inflation for the first two years, balanced by increases below inflation in the last two years, precisely in order to ease the BBC's entry into digital broadcasting. Retention of the £244 million derived from the sale of its transmitter network provided an additional cushion.

Indeed, in May 1996, when one of the BBC's most senior executives, Will Wyatt, was quizzed on *Newsnight* as to how the BBC's new digital services would be funded, he replied: "from savings we are making now, from step changes in savings we believe we can make in the future and from extra commercial money... we will be able to earn over the next ten years". Even seven months later, in the midst of a licence fee negotiation in which the BBC sought "a modest real terms increase" in its level, the BBC promised to fund the "lion's share" of its digital strategy "from increased efficiency and the contribution of its commercial arm". At this stage, of course, such proposed channels as BBC

Knowledge and BBC Choice were promised as part of the BBC's subscription partnership with Flextech, not as BBC-funded free-to-air services.

If a digital licence fee had been considered and rejected by the government at the time, it was not made evident when the 5-year settlement was announced. Yet when the BBC launched its first new digital service, a 24-hour news channel, it ran into widespread criticism: from commercial competitors, outraged that this was being offered free of charge to cable operators; from viewers, dismayed by the service's quality on air; from staff, worried by the diversion of scarce resources to a service only a minority of homes could possibly receive; and from licence fee payers, convinced that their basic services were suffering while the BBC spent twice as much – £50 million annually – on an adjunct to its news output than Sky spent on the entirety of its clearly superior news channel.

By the time the Davies Panel started receiving evidence, the issues it faced were far sharper than those Davies had considered in his 1997 pamphlet. Ironically, his co-author had re-issued much of that pamphlet – this time solely under his own name – at the beginning of 1999, even though Davies had by then apparently distanced himself from one of the options it canvassed – licence fee increases ahead of inflation. Both men attended a private seminar for the DCMS in February, where Davies made clear his preference for a digital licence fee – or so another participant in the seminar, Ray Snoddy, media editor of *The Times*, reported in his column a few days later.

The level of the fee being floated at this stage was £35, rather than the £45 posited in 1997. Yet it was not this inspired leak, but another report from Snoddy two months later, which triggered the fierce pre-publication debate that surrounded the Davies Panel. Snoddy had attended a BBC Governors' seminar on paying for broadcasting, at which Sir John Birt had – somewhat coyly – put to the attendees the view that "one of the virtues of a digital licence fee is that it falls only on those who invest in digital". Most of his audience supported the idea: thereby allowing the BBC to perform an unsubtle U-turn, which promptly alienated virtually all the commercial broadcasters (my own Channel 5 being the sole exception).

Nine major broadcast companies – soon to be joined by manufacturers and retailers – protested to Chris Smith at the potential threat to their digital investment that a supplementary licence fee represented. They quoted back at Davies – inaccurately – his previous acknowledgement that such a fee would be "a substantial disincentive to digital take-up" (in fact, he never used the word "substantial").

Interestingly, the most vociferous member of this group, BSkyB, had been immensely keen, only a little earlier, for the BBC to launch an array of subscription services which might help build the market for pay television, and also to place its existing and new free-to-air services on digital satellite as well as the digital terrestrial transmission system the BBC had championed for so long.

Now, however, Sky and its main competitor, ONdigital, had committed themselves to hefty subsidies for set-top boxes, offering them at little or no charge to new subscribers. Having themselves raised their monthly subscriptions by £2 to recoup this investment, they were distinctly unhappy about a further charge of perhaps £3 a month being imposed for what they saw as no extra benefit for consumers.

The orchestrated attack on the digital licence fee continued right up to – and beyond – publication of the Davies Report. An NOP poll was regularly quoted, suggesting that it would put 60% of consumers off digital. Even after another NOP poll showed a far lower level of resistance, this figure was still cited.

A digital licence fee was claimed to be socially divisive, hitting the poorest hardest – even though the opposite was more likely to be true, in that the poorest homes would be the least likely to adopt digital, and yet would find themselves (in the absence of a digital licence fee) paying through the basic licence fee for digital services provided free to homes which could afford pay television.

A subtler argument was that digital viewers would have more choice of viewing available, and would therefore watch the BBC less whilst having to pay more: but the same logic would lead to cable and satellite analogue customers paying a lower basic licence fee now, because on average they, too, watch less BBC output.

Another complaint was that it would be a retrospective tax for those who had already adopted digital – but the continuing surge in take-up of free decoders, after the Davies digital licence proposal had been published, suggested that advance knowledge of a possible digital surcharge would not have deterred many of those early subscribers.

The extra fee was dubbed a digital poll tax by its opponents, even though it was a voluntary charge, paid only by digital adopters, and therefore much fairer than having the overwhelming cost of the BBC's digital services paid by non-adopters. But the phrase did its intended share of damage, as did the explicit threat made by the commercial lobby that its long-term support for the basic licence fee would be jeopardised by the introduction of a digital supplement.

What Davies chose to confront in his Report was the main pre-publication thrust of the commercial lobby's attack. The fear that a digital licence fee might inhibit switching off the analogue transmission system – a clearly stated Government policy – had been raised by Davies in his own pamphlet. He now finessed the issue by devising a version of the digital licence fee that would disappear well before switch-off, by starting at a level from which it would steadily diminish until it was absorbed by the normal rise in the basic licence fee. At this point, a majority of homes would have adopted digital television, so funding additional digital services out of the general licence fee would no longer be seen as unfair.

But solving one big problem created two other small ones. For the length of time it took the basic licence fee to catch up with the digital supplement, digital homes would face no annual increase in their payments to the BBC, even though they were enjoying the improvement in quality of core BBC services that the rest of licence fee payers were funding on a rising basis year by year. Also, whatever inhibition to digital take-up there might be as a result of the digital licence fee would be maximised in the early years by the proposed structure.

In the end, the Davies Panel seemed to have spent so much effort refining its digital licence fee proposal – which even then was opposed by one member, the commercial radio boss, Lord Gordon – that it was forced to confess that it had not had time to examine the wider argument for publicly funded broadcasting.

In his foreword to the Report, Davies admitted that the Panel had been unable to define public service broadcasting or what the BBC's role should be, only that "some sort of market failure must lie at the heart of any concept of public service broadcasting". Yet no description of actual market failure was offered, though – perhaps in a nod to his old mentor, Andrew Graham – Davies did include as a final annex to the Report a brief, theoretical and unconvincing general account of market failure in broadcasting.

In practice, the Davies Report essentially attempted to deal with the BBC's bid for more resources in its own terms. Yet the BBC's evidence to the Panel was not published, nor any of the other 186 submissions: a frustrating omission. Nor was any attempt made to compare the BBC's submission with its previously published proposals and statements, even though it was clearly in sharp contrast to all that had been said to the Commons National Heritage Committee barely two years previously.

As a result, although the Report is more persuasive than its critics anticipated, it is also less impressive than it first appears. It contains 209 numbered pages, but 28 of those are blank. Indeed, excluding routine annexes, the main body of the report contains just 133 pages of text, 30 of which are the chairman's foreword, fluent and well-argued but inevitably repetitive of the main body of the report.

A further 20 pages deal somewhat inconclusively with the various licence concession schemes, and 16 pages are devoted to a skimpy section on achieving sustainability, which frankly acknowledges the weakness of the licence fee system, but does scant justice to the alternatives. Subscription is dismissed with the dubious tautology that it negates universal accessibility: but then even the one question on subscription included in the opinion survey commissioned for Davies is misleadingly summarised in the report.

There are other blemishes. Although Gavyn Davies himself is a public admirer of Sky's services, he seems to have swallowed undigested gobbets of anti-Sky propaganda. He claims in his foreword that "the majority probably have much less choice in some crucial types of programming than they had a decade ago", which is demonstrably untrue. He believes that there is "widespread resentment that the majority of the British population cannot get first-run movies on television", seemingly unaware that there has been no change in the length of time it takes for films to reach free-to-air channels: pay services simply fill a gap that has always existed in nearly all markets, but not to the detriment of free-to-air viewers.

There is also, bizarrely, on the very first page of the foreword, a seeming contradiction with the body of the Report. In his summary of his 40 recommendations, Davies says that "the prime source of new funding for extra (digital) services should be self-help (i.e., savings) by the BBC"; and that "the secondary source of new funding, amounting to about £150–200 million a year, should come from" a digital licence fee. Yet in the full Report, the Panel says that "as a broad principle, we believe the BBC should ensure that expenditure on programmes which are available only to digital viewers should be no higher than the funds generated by the digital licence fee".

This principle is enunciated no less than three times, on pages 33, 82 and 87 of the Report, along with a requirement that the BBC account annually for its success in achieving this objective. Yet on page 55 of the Report, the Panel seems to accept that, within the context of substantially upgrading all its core services, using £600 million of savings and revenue growth, the BBC should also be granted a further £150–200 million: not the £650–700 million extra it would like to spend each year on digital services, but – and crucially – over and above the £200 million it already spends.

It is very hard to reconcile that calculation on page 55 of the Report with the oft-repeated principle – which Davies himself adopted as his post-publication mantra – that it was manifestly unfair for analogue licence fee payers to subsidise digital service viewers. The Panel also adopted the principle that, in pursuit of a healthy public service broadcasting ecology, "the inherent disadvantages of the licence fee system imply that we should fund the minimum BBC services necessary to do this, not the maximum amount that could be usefully spent". The problem, as the Report ruefully admitted, is that "turning these principles into hard figures is more of an art than a science".

If we take literally the Panel's view that only temporarily and to a modest degree should new services be funded out of the basic licence fee, the implications for the BBC's digital strategy are substantial: after all, £150–200 million annually is what the BBC already spends on digital, so if that is the limit of what it can spend on new digital services, it will, as the report says, "have to prioritise its activities in the digital world and not seek automatically to expand into every new area of activity".

Was this a package the BBC could accept? Just once, immediately after the Report's publication, did the BBC unequivocally accept the principle at the heart of Davies. In an article in the Sunday Express, BBC Broadcast chief executive Will Wyatt said: "it's a tried and trusted formula. A new licence for a new level of service. Those who pay a little bit extra get a great deal more. Hence the idea for a digital licence fee, paid only by those who use digital services rather than a hike in the general fee, which would unfairly hit those who had not yet made the switch". But this unique statement of principle was thereafter buried under a formula whereby, even though the BBC recognised that a digital supplement was preferable to a rise in the basic licence fee, it was for the Government to decide what to do. The BBC would not risk short-term cash for higher principle.

Few BBC executives, other than Wyatt, found it easy to conceal the Corporation's dismay when the Davies Report was published. The Panel said that "some of the BBC's digital offerings have been distinctly threadbare" and that its future plans were "exciting" and "compelling", yet it "was not convinced by the case made by the BBC for £650 million extra funding by 2006". The main problem was that less than half that amount had been earmarked for specific proposals, and the Panel was "not happy to pre-fund services which had not yet been fully identified and specified".

The BBC complained that Davies had willed the ends but not the means by which the BBC could play a full part in the digital future. What made the pill even more bitter to swallow was that Davies also argued for a swathe of measures to ensure greater accountability for the BBC and demonstrable fairness in its trading practices. Proposals for selling off the BBC's production resources and 49% of its commercial division, BBC Worldwide, were especially unwelcome to the Corporation.

But the BBC's disappointment did nothing to assuage the commercial lobby. The Report's rejection of advertising on the BBC, and recognition of their anxieties on BBC accountability and fair trading, were poor compensation for the survival of the hated digital licence fee – even though it started at £24 a year, a far lower level than they had expected; even though it diminished to £12, so averaging just £19 during its life before eventually disappearing; and even though it could have only the most minimal impact on analogue switch-off.

The Sun headlined "Fury at Beeb's £19 'Digi-tax'". The fury was largely their own – "scandalous" was the verdict – "a stitch-up", "a scam". *The Mirror* – though it was about to close its loss-making television subsidiary – pronounced the digital licence fee "outrageous". Even the *Daily Mail* – only a marginal investor in commercial television – described it as "an insult to the public's intelligence". Its columnist, Andrew Neil, harking back to the original Davies pamphlet, funded by the BBC, and the known political connections, described the report as "about as 'independent' as *Pravda* was in the Soviet era". The digital licence fee was a poll-tax, a luddite levy, ludicrous and unfair: and the Report itself should be consigned "to the waste basket".

The Sun fulminated that "the digital poll tax is supported by no newspaper of any consequence", thereby putting in their place *The Independent On Sunday, The Financial Times, The Guardian* and its own stable mate, *The Times*. The commercial broadcasters redoubled their efforts, with Sky's top two executives, Carlton Television's chief executive, United Broadcasting's chief executive and Granada's chief executive all placing lengthy newspaper articles condemning the digital licence fee.

New arguments joined the old ones. The BBC needed no new money in order to run its digital channels – it could easily tighten its belt. Brussels would object to state funding that would distort the digital market. A digital licence fee would be a liability if it were introduced (as recommended) just before the May 2000 local elections. Misreading a consultant's report submitted by the BBC to Davies, the commercial lobbyists claimed that London

Economics had demonstrated how the colour TV licence had delayed the switch-off of 405-line transmissions by 2–4 years.

In fact, the London Economics document simply showed that even if the colour licence revenue had not been spent on programming, it would in theory have caused only a modest delay in 405-line switch-off. That the revenue was used to fund BBC2 and convert BBC1 into colour was clearly an immense driver of 625-line take-up: a fact conveniently ignored by the commercial lobbyists.

In response, Davies penned a series of letters and articles in which he sharpened his critique of their stance. In his Report, he had pointed out that "the private broadcasters who are opposed to a digital licence supplement are in the position of arguing simultaneously that the new technologies will open a new world, offering a compelling uplift in service provision, and that a (monthly) supplement of £1.57 on the licence fee will kill the new technology. We are more inclined to believe the former than the latter".

Now he went further, arguing that leaving the licence fee settlement untouched, and funding BBC digital services from a digital supplement, would save the analogue licence fee payer £10 a year in digital costs and a further £25 over seven years in lower licence fee levels: all of which may have been implicit in his report, but was invisible in its summary. And he seized on a further piece of BBC consultant's research, from a company called .econ, which took the London Economics argument a step further.

This document predicted that pay television services would carry digital penetration no further than 60–65% of homes. A mass of consumers would only convert to digital if there were additional free-to-air services on offer – and the kind of services the public apparently wanted were the kind the BBC tended to provide. So, argued Davies, in the interests of driving the analogue switch-off the commercial broadcasters claimed was in their interest and the national interest, they should support the BBC's investment in digital.

But his critics were not convinced that BBC free-to-air channels would help drive the digital market. Sky, in particular, produced evidence that BBC channels did not feature in the top ten reasons offered by consumers for going digital. On that basis, it was reasonable to propose that either the BBC should offer such services only in subscription form, so that viewers could decide for themselves whether or not to pay for them; or they should be funded out of direct taxation if they were perceived as some form of public welfare; or they should not be offered at all.

This last option, however, was never publicly adopted by the commercial lobby. If the BBC wanted to provide additional, digital free-to-air services, let it do so: it should simply be held to its promise to fund them from internal savings and commercial revenues, even if this was unfair to analogue licence fee payers.

Nor did they accept that the digital licence fee could be fairly compared with the colour licence. With colour, the supplementary fee was admittedly 100%, but the increase in the number of channels funded by it was 50%. The digital supplement might add only 20% to the cost of a licence fee, but it would increase by less than 5% the number of channels, and none would have the broad appeal of BBC2.

Nor were the commercial operators prepared to accept the London Economics argument that the impact of a digital licence fee on digital take-up would possibly be positive rather than negative, in supporting BBC digital spending. They commissioned yet another consultant's report, from NERA (an economic consulting firm), who unsurprisingly supported their clients' preconceptions. NERA claimed that a digital licence fee would delay analogue switch-off by about three years because it would reduce the take-up of digital television by between two million and 5.7 million homes in the period 2004–2008, costing broadcasters, manufacturers and retailers nearly £5 billion.

Davies derided these figures. If a temporary £2 a month – reducing annually – surcharge for digital would do so much damage, why did Sky and ONdigital voluntarily increase their charges by £2 a month on a permanent basis earlier this year? Were they trying to destroy their businesses? And if it would have such a damaging effect, would it not make economic sense for the industry to pay the charge itself?

Yet the political tide appeared to be turning. Ray Snoddy reported a possible arrangement whereby the Government would drop the digital licence fee in exchange for the commercial broadcasters supporting an increase in the basic licence fee. A member of the Davies Panel, the economist Lord Lipsey, protested at such a deal in a letter to *The Times* at the end of September.

> It would transfer the whole cost of developing the BBC's new digital services from digital subscribers who benefit from them to licence payers generally who do not. Since on average ordinary licence fee-payers are less well-off than those who have gone digital, this would be Robin Hood in reverse – the poorer robbed to subsidise the richer. I cannot believe that this Government would contemplate appeasing the digital lobby at the cost of such social regressiveness.

Within a week, the first inspired leaks began to appear. "Blair set to block £24 'poll tax' on digital TVs", announced *The Mail On Sunday* at the beginning of October. The same day, *Sunday Business* reported that Chris Smith was calling in the rival digital broadcasters to insist that they co-operate in order to help speed digital take-up: the price they might have to pay, perhaps, for the dropping of the digital licence fee. A fortnight later, *The Sunday Times* headline read "TV licence fee to rise as digital levy is axed", quoting "senior Whitehall sources" as saying it was easier to raise an existing fee than introduce a new one. A Davies Panel member was reported as saying that "Chris Smith has been got at".

Less than a week later, the other shoe dropped. *The Express* reported that the licence fee would rise by £10, but that pensioners would get free licences in order to make the increase politically acceptable. "Ministers" were now quoted as saying it was easier to raise an existing fee than introduce a new one. Chris Smith, it was reported, "believes that a modest licence fee rise is the ideal solution, provided pensioners are exempt".

The Times carried a similar story as its front page lead. A DCMS minister was quoted as saying: "do Governments introduce new taxes before general elections? – no, successful Governments do not". Both Chris Smith and his junior broadcasting minister were said to believe that "increasing the standard licence fee would be a more acceptable way of raising money for the BBC", provided pensioners were not hit.

Another week, another set of headlines, as Chris Smith installed a team of auditors in the BBC to check whether its claims for extra digital funding were justified. Some saw this as a snub to Davies, though he had called for just such an investigation in his report. Chris Smith denied it was a prelude to dropping the digital licence fee.

Two weeks later, however, the Chancellor of the Exchequer duly announced that pensioners over 75 would be granted free TV licences, at a cost over £300 million a year. This sum shocked the chairman of the Royal Commission on long-term care for the elderly. He felt that it was a gimmick which was "about as much use as toffee apples" for pensioners, who would be much better off if given the money directly and left to decide for themselves if free television was their priority. The announcement was also criticised as endangering the supposed independence of BBC domestic broadcasting from Government finance.

Nonetheless, the ground seemed to be prepared for dropping the most contentious and most important recommendation in the Davies Report. Davies himself claims that the issue is still open and that he will be personally involved in sifting all the responses to his recommendations, the deadline for which passed at the beginning of November. A decision will be made early in 2000.

Meanwhile, the publication of the BBC's response to Davies at last allowed us to see the scale of its ambitions. Astonishingly, it renewed its bid for a 30% increase in spending by 2006: over £700 million a year. Cunningly, it buried its digital plans within an overall scheme for investing in all kinds of new content for existing as well as new services, under the headings of creativity, learning and citizenship.

It completely ignored the question of why some of its new digital channels could not be subscription-funded, as was originally planned. Yet again, it falsely asserted that subscription services concentrate on films, sport and adult entertainment, ignoring the fact that 85% of viewing to subscription channels is not to those genres, and that two of the most popular subscription channels offer general entertainment – Sky One and UK Gold, which is scheduled by the BBC.

The document opposed a digital licence fee if the intention was to phase it out. As for its level, there was no reason why it should not be £48 a year rather than £24 – in fact, the implication of the BBC's spending plans would put the level at £72, or £30 on the basic licence fee. With its talk of BBC Open Centres in every high street and banks of educational content, it seemed to assume that the best way of funding major public investments in the social fabric of the country was through a semi-accountable broadcaster funded by a flat-rate household tax. Not surprisingly, Ray Snoddy in *The Times* urged that "the BBC proposals should be rejected as outrageous".

The Davies Report, fluent and intelligent though it is, seems to have been outflanked by the limitations of its remit. Unable to conduct a thorough investigation into the BBC, let alone public service broadcasting and the wider broadcasting industry, it could only follow a narrow logic which the BBC response sought to by-pass, saying that "the digital supplement recommended by the Panel...will clearly not even meet the current costs of the BBC's services, let alone enable enhancements to them".

A major inquiry, Chris Smith told Gavyn Davies, would not be appropriate till 2003/4, in advance of BBC Charter review. By then, of course, the die will have been cast as to what kind of BBC we have, and what part it will play in the digital future. The Davies Report, for all its merits, appears to have been an opportunity missed.

If the central recommendation of the Davies Report is rejected, it will join the four other major post-war Reports in such a fate. Beveridge urged retention of the BBC's monopoly, Pilkington wholesale reform of ITV, Annan an Open Broadcasting Authority to operate the fourth channel and Peacock a switch to subscription funding for the BBC. All the big ideas fell by the wayside, for good reasons or bad – though Davies was willing to concede that Peacock may yet prove right on subscription.

Fifty years on from Beveridge, broadcasting policy is still determined more by the ebb and flow of politics, and the activities of determined pressure groups, than by ad hoc committees of the great and the good, however politically well-connected, and however cogent their recommendations. Indeed, it could be argued that the Hunt Report, skimpy as it was, was the most successful in seeing its ideas implemented – not least because they reflected the prejudices of the Government of the day.

Of course, the fate of the Davies Report is not yet sealed, and many of its recommendations in relation to BBC accountability and fair trading may yet prove significant. Even if Davies loses the argument on the digital licence fee, the persisting injustice to analogue licence fee payers of funding the minority of households able to enjoy the BBC's digital offerings may yet trigger a consumer revolt that causes the BBC and the Government great difficulty.

Meanwhile, the BBC sails on, like a great ship of state, shrugging off the Davies Report arguments, bidding for vast increases in its already huge income, and preparing to be both school and citizens advice bureau in the digital age. Perhaps in fifty years time, its response to Davies will seem as other-worldly and anachronistic as its evidence to Beveridge fifty years ago. From John Reith to Greg Dyke is a remarkable journey to have travelled. There is a long way to go yet.

[8]
The BBC in the Digital Century

10 February 2000

The long aftermath of the Davies Report coincided with a changing of the guard at the BBC. As ministers – and ministries – debated the merits of the Davies conclusions, and as the commercial digital operators worked themselves to fever pitch in their opposition to a digital licence fee, the Governors embarked on the slow process of transferring power to a commercially-astute multi-millionaire who had never spent a day working at the BBC. His would be the decisive voice in readying the corporation for the digital century: and his biggest challenge would be dealing with his formidable predecessor's legacy.

At the end of January, 2000, when John Birt left the BBC, he had spent four years as Deputy Director-General and nine as Director-General, the longest stint as DG since John Reith himself. Like Reith, but in some ways even more remarkably for having come in from the outside, he imposed his personality on the institution. Dissent from within became as absent as in Reith's day. Like Reith, and like no other DG, Birt earned a knighthood whilst in office. Like Reith, he was eventually eased out of office, if only by a couple of months – and the peerage that induced his early departure, in being announced whilst he was still in situ, edged him a notch ahead of Reith, the only other DG to have reached the House of Lords.

Though he starts his career in the upper house on the crossbenches, perhaps, like Reith, Birt dreams of a Cabinet post in due course. After all, his former co-editor of the ITV current affairs series *World In Action*, Gus Macdonald, has already secured a seat at that most elevated table, along with his own peerage. With so many media folk now cramming the New Labour benches in the Lords – Waheed Alli, Richard Attenborough, Melvyn Bragg, Clive Hollick and David Puttnam alongside Macdonald – it is not thought improper or even unusual for the former guardians of strict impartiality to serve the government of the day. Birt's successor as editor-in-chief at the BBC personally donated over £50,000 to the Labour Party and its leadership less than five years before his controversial appointment to that position.

Like his two predecessors, Alasdair Milne and Michael Checkland, Birt was an Oxford graduate. All were awarded honorary fellowships by their respective colleges whilst in office, thus sustaining the close relationship between the university and public service broadcasting: the President of Magdalen and the Master of Balliol have both served on the Channel 4 board, as well as being influential commentators on broadcasting policy.

Milne and Checkland shared another distinction: both were dislodged by the same chairman – Marmaduke Hussey – in favour of their deputies. Checkland replaced Milne and Birt in turn replaced Checkland. Perhaps reflecting on these precedents, Birt subsequently pushed out the Deputy Director-General he had personally brought in from ITV, Bob Phillis, and ruled thereafter without a deputy. He also managed to survive a shoot-out with Hussey after their relationship deteriorated into hostility and lengthy silence. Hussey's successor as chairman of the BBC was, conveniently, Sir Christopher Bland, who had been Birt's chairman when he had been London Weekend Television's

Director of Programmes in the 1980s. To complete the symmetry, Birt's successor in the LWT job, Greg Dyke, now took over from him at the BBC.

Dyke dutifully paid tribute to Birt, not least for his supposedly "brilliant" positioning of the BBC for the digital age. Yet Birt's legacy, after a near-decade of upheaval, is an equivocal one, and the claims made for his incumbency are already in question. In the context of this series of lectures, the issues of importance are not so much of internal structure but of legitimacy, of accountability, of funding, of distinctiveness: indeed, of the role and justification for the public sector in broadcasting – in particular, the BBC.

The first claim made on Birt's behalf is that he saved the BBC from the privatisation a Thatcherite Conservative party might have desired. Even David Mellor, the broadcasting minister who steered the 1990 Act onto the statute book asserted this in a live BBC radio discussion of Birt's reign two days before his final departure. Certainly, as a previous lecture has described, some of Mrs Thatcher's more radical ministers were prone to rushes of blood to the head, as exemplified by Lord Young's short-lived attempt to exile BBC2 to near invisibility in a purely satellite-delivered distribution mode.

Equally beyond dispute is that Birt's first priority as Deputy Director-General had been to impose strict editorial discipline on the BBC's television current affairs output, culminating in that department's merger with news, so re-creating the powerful internal empire that had been Hugh Greene's stepping-stone to the top thirty years earlier. The control Birt exercised alienated a raft of long-serving BBC staff, as did his subsequent structural reforms, powerfully spun by Birt's many dozens of corporate affairs publicists (or "thought police" in BBC vernacular) as evidence of the Corporation embracing the processes of the market. That it was Birt's predecessor, Michael Checkland, who introduced the process of reform and cost-savings that became known as "producer choice" has long been air-brushed from history.

The heavy hand of Birt on the editorial tiller may have helped fend off Tory hard-liners in the late 1980s, but the fact is that Peacock had put paid to any privatisation agenda before Birt even joined the BBC, and by the time Birt became Director-General, it was John Major, not Margaret Thatcher, who was Prime Minister. The Secretaries of State in Major's new Department of National Heritage were no threat to the BBC: Mellor himself, Peter Brooke, Stephen Dorrell and Virginia Bottomley. Birt certainly worked hard to persuade ministers to the BBC's view of the world, securing renewal of the BBC's Charter and regular increases in the licence fee: but there was little contrary pressure, and the BBC's PR successes do not, in retrospect, seem all that clever.

For instance, the BBC lobbied hard – to the point of misleading Parliament – to "protect" (in BBC-speak) certain sporting events from exclusive coverage on pay television. A BBC-inspired Lords rebellion imposed a listed events clause on the 1996 Broadcasting Act. But in the process, the BBC so alienated the cricket authorities – who were the prime financial victims of this unsought protection – that when Channel 4 mounted a determined onslaught on the Test Match contract, the BBC suffered an humiliating rejection.

Similarly, the BBC's obsession with gatekeeper issues in the digital pay-tv environment alternately irritated the government and provoked it into legislative action: but in the event no abuse materialised, and the public money spent by the BBC's chairman on a cod video warning of likely BSkyB misbehaviour turned out to be an expensive own goal.

Even the BBC's pressure for the launch of digital terrestrial television – successful as it was in shaping policy – has proved partially counter-productive. The method of allocating frequencies so as to create six DTT multiplexes was designed to maximise short-term take-up of digital, but has in practice made much more difficult the long-term objective of switching off the analogue terrestrial transmission system. The frequency specialists are still puzzling over a solution. And the huge expense of running a DTT system in parallel to analogue for twenty years will add billions to the cost of going digital, with only marginal benefits.

If hindsight has taken some of the gloss from the BBC's successful management of its Whitehall relationships, there can be no doubting the skill with which the BBC has harnessed academic, political and editorial opinion in defence of the concept of public service broadcasting, and of the BBC's role in providing it. Even here, though, the BBC's short term success may prove to be a long-term error.

The most influential writer in this specialist area has been Andrew Graham, whose views were most fully outlined in the 65-page pamphlet he co-authored in 1997 with fellow-economist Gavyn Davies, who subsequently chaired the government-appointed Panel that reported on the funding of the BBC in 1999. In assessing the significance of this pamphlet in the previous lecture, attention was focused on the provenance of the case for a digital licence fee, which Davies rehearsed for the first time there, and on the proposition of spiralling absurdity that, the greater the danger that the BBC's share of viewing might decline, the higher the licence fee needed to be raised to offset such danger. Shades of Reith's "brute force of monopoly"!

That it was Graham who contributed most to this formulation was confirmed when much of the pamphlet's content re-appeared in 1999 under his sole authorship in a set of essays by ten economists on funding the BBC. Both publications had been commissioned and paid for by the BBC, so it is no surprise to find virtually near-unanimous belief that the market cannot be trusted, the public sector is vital, the BBC is the best defence against market distortions and the licence fee is the best way of funding public sector broadcasting.

By 1999, as it happens, Davies had concluded that open-ended increases in the licence fee were wholly unrealistic politically, which may account for his ceasing to be a co-author with Graham. In any event, his chairmanship of the BBC funding panel would have made re-statement of his 1997 position somewhat awkward. But what is perhaps more significant is that the Davies Report nonetheless subsequently replicated in large measure Graham's exposition of supposed market failure.

Graham asks three questions of the market in broadcasting. How well will it serve the public interest? Will it help shape a democratic environment? And will it extend rather than diminish individual experience? No doubt, if Graham asked the same questions about the British press, he would conclude that, as the market clearly has weaknesses, there should be public sector newspaper publishing. That virtually any devotee of freedom of the press outside Beijing would recoil with horror at the thought of publicly-funded newspapers barely registers in the Graham approach. Nor is there any recognition of the fact that the public sector in broadcasting exists as a result of technical constraints, rather than a considered response to demonstrable market failure.

Most of the economists included in these publications subscribe to the truism that broadcasting is a public good, in the sense that one person's consumption is not at the expense of any other person's consumption. Some also go on to argue that quality broadcasting is a merit good, in that – without the right economic structure – consumers might buy less of it than they should. So a licence fee system of funding has the virtue of creating quality broadcasting that might not otherwise exist, in the absence of a mechanism that forces a flat-rate payment by consumers, and thereafter entails no further payment for additional consumption.

It is hard to see why the same arguments, again, should not apply to the press: the marginal cost of any additional copy of a newspaper is virtually nil, as with transmission of programmes to additional viewers. A newspaper of unimpeachable quality might well be created by public funding – even a forced flat-rate tax on all readers of newspapers. But no-one in a free society would have the foolhardiness to suggest such a course of action.

Indeed, the proponents of the licence fee, in their enthusiasm for what they describe as broadcasting free at the point of consumption, seem scarcely to notice that the first moment of broadcasting consumption is actually rather expensive, at over £100, even if all subsequent moments may be free. That it is broadcasting funded out of general taxation which might more accurately be described as "free at the point of consumption" does not diminish the general enthusiasm for the licence fee.

The sophistry of Graham's line of argument becomes clear when his actual questions are examined. Not, "is the market relatively successful?", but "will the market produce all that is desired?" – a question that could be asked of any number of markets without arriving at the conclusion that what is needed is high levels of public funding.

He adduces as a further example of market failure that broadcasting can have adverse "external effects" – such as amplifying violence in society. Yet there is no evidence that BBC broadcasting is immune from such effects itself, let alone that the BBC's presence in the market diminishes the flow or consequences of such effects from other suppliers.

He believes that community feelings, cultures and values may be undermined by "the fragmentation of audiences that purely commercial broadcasting may produce". Yet the intervention of licence-fee funded services in the market can only further fragment the audience – unless mathematics as well as logic is being stood on its head. Nor will everyone subscribe to the notion that mass audiences are inherently socially virtuous. That more people may have experienced and discussed certain transmissions simply because there was no other choice is scarcely evidence that those programmes, let alone those experiences and discussions, were of some special higher value. That phenomenon was simply a function of spectrum scarcity.

Rather more alarming is Graham's assertion that "in a democratic society it is undesirable that the mass media should be entirely in private control". Unless – which must be doubted – he is advocating state-funded newspapers, he is evidently using the phrase "mass media" where he means broadcasting, and also confusing the concept of private control with profit-maximisation. The Scott Trust controls *The Guardian* and *The Observer*, exercising a substantially more vigorous defence of the citizen than the state-owned BBC can muster, yet it operates in a market environment and displays impressive commercial skills.

Graham goes on to assert that "it is not the private market which has given the UK a broadcasting industry which is widely regarded as the best in the world": a line of argument that Edmund Burke might have admired, but which is essentially deploying the accidental facts of history as if they were the outcome of many failed experiments succeeded by a single successful one.

Graham's attempts to support his theoretical framework with practical arguments are undermined by his evident ignorance of the real world of broadcasting. Because the BBC is a particularly expensive producer of programmes, he believes all programme production must be very expensive, so creating a barrier to entry into the market-place. He is wrong.

He believes the fixed costs of renting space on satellites is high, creating a further barrier. He is wrong. He believes the BBC spends more per capita on training than its commercial rivals. He is wrong. He believes the cost of rights and talent is inexorably rising, particularly in sport. Some costs are, but by no means all: he is wrong, again. He believes that because the biggest broadcast companies are growing larger and regularly merge, consumer choice is bound to diminish. In fact, there have been many new entrants to the broadcast market, large, medium-sized and small, greatly enlarging choice: wrong yet again.

Graham is convinced that "gateway" systems, especially BSkyB's, are a threat to choice – dishes, decoders, electronic programme guides, subscriber management centres and encryption technology. He likens the digital world to "being able to shop at Tesco, but only at Tesco". In fact, successive investigations by the Office of Fair Trading having found no discrimination against Sky's competitors, and the combination of regulatory requirements and market imperatives has made access to satellite broadcasting remarkably easy.

Graham is not only wrong, but seems entirely ignorant – or forgetful – of the stream of abuses of its dominant position that characterised the BBC's behaviour for decades, and continues to linger. It is, moreover, somewhat ironic that the main current preoccupation of the government in managing the timetable for analogue switch-off is the multiplicity of choice for the consumer in the digital market-place, and the incompatibility of the hardware used by different populations across the different digital platforms – satellite, terrestrial and cable.

Graham also ignores all the evidence that every expansion of the broadcast market has led to improvements in quality as well as in choice. His version of broadcast economics allows him to imagine that, because "more channels fragment audiences", so the average cost of programmes must rise. By this syllogistic means, he concludes that "choice has a cost in broadcasting" and that "under free market conditions, consumers will face a choice between a narrower range of cheaper (and yet still high quality) broadcasting and a broader range of more expensive and yet lower quality programming". He even offers a technical explanation for the process: the problem of "externalities" – caused by fragmentation, in that "the person who migrates away from existing channels in favour of others imposes a cost on all those who do not move".

Yet this is demonstrably false of the BBC – the size of its audience bears no relation to its income, and therefore has no impact on its costs. Departing BBC viewers impose no costs on remaining ones. And the argument even fails to apply to the commercial market.

In fact, the expansion of the market has brought new money into broadcasting: more advertising revenue and – for the first time – subscription funds. Just as has happened in the US, the declining audience share of the networks has been accompanied by an increase in their advertising revenues (as advertisers better understand the value of network airtime) and so an increase in their programme investment. ITV has lost a quarter of its audience in the last eight years, but its revenue increases have accelerated: though, to be fair, ITV is cushioned from the full impact of market forces by a protective regulatory framework.

The market has delivered to the consumer more choice of programmes, more high-cost programmes as well as more low-cost (and recycled) programmes, more choice of levels of spend, and more value at every level of spend. Reality could not be more diametrically opposed to Graham's imagined outcome.

Graham believes that, because of their intrinsic quality, the UK's television programmes achieve export sales levels above those of the US – whereas in fact they trail far behind. And, far from the UK's exports – such as they are – being led by the BBC's public service ethos, the single most important factor underpinning UK sales is actually the very success of the Americans, who have created a powerful demand for English-language programming, thanks to the well-developed facilities for dubbing English soundtracks that US dominance of the market has generated.

He also seems to believe that the BBC is more trusted as a news source than its competitors – whereas many years of research by the IBA and ITC have established that the BBC is less trusted than ITN and even Sky News. And he suggests that television viewers are prone simultaneously to be ignorant of what is available and unwilling to sample anything new – both false. He confidently asserts that "it is difficult to see how both profitability and responsibility can be constant strategic aims at the same time". The notion that profitability (let alone survival) might depend upon responsibility seems never to have occurred to him.

Graham concludes that he has provided "a strong case for thinking that broadcasting should not be left just to the market". Others might disagree. Not that no such case for public intervention in the market can be made: only that his version weakens rather than strengthens that case. But the worst consequences of Graham's spreading influence in policy circles are that his faulty demonstration of market failure has been allowed to serve as a given, and that he has further woven into the case for public service broadcasting the doubtful proposition that its essential funding mechanism is the licence fee.

Indeed, just as the BBC has, under John Birt, hardened its opposition to any other form of funding than the licence fee, so a cadre of well-meaning economists – by no means all Labour sympathisers like Graham – have followed Graham in assessing (however inadequately) the various forms of funding and plumped for the licence fee.

It was not until the Davies Panel assembled the market failure arguments in Annex VIII of their Report that finally the emperor's clothes were exposed to comprehensive challenge. Davies had, by his own admission, failed to provide any proper analysis of the case for public service broadcasting, blaming lack of time. He relied entirely on the premise that "some sort of market failure must lie at the heart of any concept of public service broadcasting": indeed, "it is impossible to argue for a public service broadcaster unless market failure can be shown".

What Davies could not do was just that. Annex VIII lists the six different reasons why market failure arises in broadcasting, but at no point showed why the provision of public service broadcasting by the BBC, let alone on the current scale and at the current cost, even less at a higher cost, was the best or only way of curing potential market failure.

The only one of the responses to the Davies Report published in November 1999 that addressed the issue of market failure was that from BSkyB. But even BSkyB did not issue a detailed critique of Annex VIII until December 1999. It clearly carries the imprint of the research consultancy led by Bill Bishop, co-author with Cento Veljanovski of the robust paper from the Institute of Economic Affairs that had excoriated the weak logic in the 1982 Hunt Report.

The critique carefully refutes the six Davies arguments for market failure in turn: that broadcasting is a public good; that quality broadcasting is a merit good; that consumers are not fully informed; that broadcasting produces externalities; that economies of scale exist in broadcasting: and that there is spectrum scarcity. The document persuasively shows that either the supposed failure is immaterial; or that it appears in many other contexts without harmful consequences or state interference; or that there are ways of correcting potential market failure without the need for a publicly funded broadcaster, especially on the scale of the BBC; or that extra funds for the BBC will not correct the failure; or that the Davies Report is simply factually incorrect.

The document's conclusion is low-key, but nonetheless devastating: "the analysis of market failure included in the Panel's Report simply shows that the conditions required for a market to function optimally might not hold in relation to the provision of broadcasting services – this is not normally, however, considered to justify government intervention, particularly in the form of publicly funded service provision".

Deprived of its patina of academic credibility as the necessary answer to market failure, the BBC's difficulties in demonstrating its legitimacy become all the more apparent. In the age of spectrum scarcity, it had been a commonplace that precious transmission frequencies should be managed by government, and only handed out to reputable and regulated broadcasters, accepting different levels of public obligation. The regulatory regime that characterised ITV – and that had so dismayed the commercial lobbyists of the 1950's – eroded the exclusive claim of the BBC to public service status. The launch of Channel 4 in 1982 posed an even greater challenge.

Here, after all, was a commercial broadcaster, entirely funded by advertisers, but which had no private shareholders, paid no dividends, sought no profits that could not be ploughed back into programmes, and consciously addressed minority audiences in a way that BBC1, in particular, could not match. And for all Channel 4's outspokenness, it was consistently perceived by the public – according to ITC research over the years – as less biased than the BBC.

Indeed, the BBC's reputation for impartiality – especially in dealing with its own affairs – has suffered a series of blows. A recent documentary series on its history, made by an independent producer, concluded with an extended paean of praise for the licence fee from one of the BBC's own presenters, Sue Lawley, all the more puzzling for having no connection to the preceding narrative. When the BBC launched its pay-television joint venture, UK TV, its own media correspondent reported as fact – not just as the BBC's claim – that licence revenue was not involved: a contentious and almost certainly untrue statement.

The BBC was also fiercely partisan in lobbying for the listed sports events legislation – an approach that spilled over into its own coverage of an issue it had almost single-handedly created. More recently, a group of BBC journalists published a letter deploring BSkyB's attacks on the BBC's *News 24* service: a doubtful exercise of their obligations to impartiality made all the more reprehensible for slavishly reproducing the misleading arguments invented by the BBC's own corporate publicists. Perhaps most controversial of all has been the lavish spending of licence fee funds on publicity campaigns, on and off air, falsely describing the licence fee as the "only" way of funding specific kinds of BBC programming.

Another of the BBC's claims for special public service status was its commitment to universality – the availability of BBC services to the whole of the UK, free at the point of use. This has become a particular BBC mantra, deployed as much to justify the licence fee as to define the BBC's public service role. As we have seen, the Annan Committee saw a clear link between universal availability and the licence fee, and opposed the BBC's local radio strategy because a significant proportion of licence fee payers would be unable to gain access to local services.

Yet universality of availability of signal applies as much to the ITV system and Channel 4 as to the BBC: the differential costs of transmission to remote areas are absorbed into the economic arrangements for the commercial broadcasters, effectively as part of their licence obligations. Channel 5, as it happens, is excused such an obligation because suitable frequencies cannot be made available: but those cable companies that wish to enjoy exclusivity in given franchise areas must commit to building out their systems in a set time-frame as the price of local monopoly.

What emerges is that previous definitions of public service status – universality, impartiality, absence of the profit motive and special content – are not the BBC's exclusive preserve. Not surprisingly, in the early years of the Birt incumbency, a determined effort was made by the BBC to find other ways of describing its distinctiveness. After all, if the market was obstinately declining to exhibit the standard symptoms of market failure, the BBC needed to demonstrate what the audience would lose if it were less well or securely funded, or if it disappeared.

The problem with this approach was that great swathes of BBC television output – excellent as it might be – were indistinguishable from the offerings of the commercial players. This is not surprising: after all, the creative community is not a BBC preserve, and the emergence of the independent sector has allowed talent to escape from the protective but restrictive relationships with broadcasters.

The BBC has had to fall back on certain types of programmes and peak-time scheduling of minority-interest material as its definition of its distinctiveness. Yet consumers are rarely asked whether they believe that the difference between having forty minutes of *Panorama* at 10pm on a Monday, rather than fifty minutes of *Tonight* With Trevor Macdonald at 10pm on a Thursday, is worth £2.2 billion per annum of public money.

Radio, of course, is different: the BBC, out of the television licence, invests in its radio services 85% of all radio spend in the UK. The commercial sector, whilst growing, cannot compete with this non-market behaviour. But it is not its radio distinctiveness that can legitimise the BBC's exclusive access to a licence fee that falls as a compulsory flat charge on all television households.

Briefly, Birt flirted with a high ground approach, aiming to drive the quality of BBC television out of reach of its competitors, even at the expense of audience share. But this Himalayan option was quietly discarded as the reality was confronted: a precipitate decline in viewership would threaten the BBC's funding. After all, if everyone was obliged to pay the licence fee, they were entitled to the full range of programmes – popular as well as minority, *EastEnders* as well as *Horizon*, the *National Lottery* as well as *Omnibus*. And if audience share dropped too far, then viewers might revolt against the licence fee system. The BBC had to tread a delicate line: distinctive enough to justify a licence fee, but not so distinctive as to undermine it.

Indeed, the licence fee, which the BBC has justified as the least-worst way of providing secure funding as well as operational independence, is a tricky beast to ride. It is, by definition, regressive: charged at a flat rate, irrespective of ability to pay or the number of television sets in a household. Its level and its impact are immune to consumers' views as to the worth of BBC output. It gives viewers no choice, yet imposes on the BBC imagined obligations which may not match the preferences of those who pay it. Not surprisingly, independent surveys show that only about a third of viewers are content with the licence fee system.

A further difficulty is that the licence fee implies a degree of accountability that the BBC fails to deliver, despite a constant flow of supposed surrogates for accountability. There are public consultations on possible changes of policy or new initiatives: but these are skimpy and unconvincing, and no single example exists of a change or initiative being abandoned as a result of such consultation.

Town hall meetings, appearances by top executives before Parliamentary committees, lengthy negotiations with ministers and civil servants, annual reports and annual pledges: all these exist, yet the trappings of accountability fail to convince. The BBC's Governors are overwhelmingly seen as both too close to the corporation's executive decisions and too little able to influence them.

The Davies Report recommended a range of measures to impose more financial accountability on the BBC, and re-opened an issue identified fifty years ago by the Beveridge Committee in calling for a secretariat solely serving the Board of Governors so as to enable them to scrutinise the actions of the executive in an informed manner. Whether there is such an inclination, of course, must be open to doubt. The BBC's annual reports offer numerous examples of individual governors risking ridicule by solemnly reciting BBC nostrums, such as that licence fee funds are not put at risk in BBC commercial ventures, or that the BBC operates strictly according to meaningful fair trading rules.

Not surprisingly, despite many years of trying to persuade the public of its commitment to accountability, the BBC was forced to admit in its 1999 annual report that just 34% actually believed it to be an accountable organisation – though that fact was so deeply buried in the text, and so devoid of comment, that only the most eagle-eyed reader would have spotted it. Far greater prominence was given to a series of "we will do better" pledges as vacuous as they were beyond measurement – such as "we promise to offer the best value for money"; or "we promise to provide programmes that are valued by everyone"; or – most amusingly – "we promise to be open and accountable".

That there is an obvious financial mechanism for delivering real accountability has not eluded the BBC. As subscription and other forms of transaction funding spread their way into the broadcasting market-place, the BBC is inexorably reminded of the licence fee's origins: as a subscription paid only by those using the BBC's services. It was the introduction in 1955 of non-BBC services that broke this simple, logical link. The BBC's rhetorical assault on the notion of subscription funding has intensified as the case for switching to it has strengthened.

The main argument used is that subscription funding would undermine the BBC's universality. But this would only be meaningful if the licence fee inflicted no cost on the consumer. The BBC's universality is a function of its transmitter system and the legal requirement for any consumer of any television services to pay a subscription – sorry, licence fee – to the BBC. Not forcing people to pay for services they might choose to do without in no way reduces the universal availability of the BBC: only, potentially, its universal take-up.

Some economists criticise subscription in theoretical terms because, almost by definition, whatever level of charge is set for a subscriber service, there will be some consumers excluded by price, even though their willingness to pay for the service may exceed the marginal cost of supplying it. This technical inefficiency is shared, of course, by virtually all products in the market place. By comparison, the licence fee is efficient in economic terms, but only if the compulsion and inequity involved in the licence fee system are ignored, let alone the high costs – some £250 million per annum – of collection and evasion, which in turn compound the unfair impact on honest households of paying yet more for BBC services they might be willing to do without.

It is not just the lack of choice and accountability which make the licence fee so suspect. In his first formal interview as Director-General, Greg Dyke had told Sir David Frost that he supported the licence fee because it favoured the poor, guaranteeing them – and not just the rich – quality services. He later amplified this notion: "at one time, I believed that once subscription was available in every home, it would be difficult to justify the licence fee; however, over time, I have come to the conclusion that making some services universally available to all, rich or poor, is more important".

Just three years earlier, in fact, Dyke had described the licence fee as "a poll-tax difficult to justify when there are literally dozens of channels available" – but that was before he became a candidate for Director-General. To that end, it is understandable that he should, for instance, acknowledge the likelihood of medium-term survival of the licence fee when being interviewed by a selection panel with well-established prejudices. But to abandon the clear superiority of subscription as a method of funding the BBC in favour of the licence fee, for such inadequate and illogical reasons, is disappointing.

After all, it is the poor – especially the honest poor – who bear the heaviest burden of the licence fee's unfairness. Subscription systems typically charge on a per-set, not a per-home basis. The average number of sets per UK home is just under three. If payment for the BBC's services were charged per set – which would be possible if all homes received BBC television through a decoder – then homes with just one set could expect a substantial reduction in the fee paid. Far from the licence fee protecting the poor, it forces them – under penalty of prosecution – to subsidise the rich, who not only are better able to afford the uniform flat fee, but are far more likely to possess several sets.

As for the universal availability argument, that has been overtaken by technological advances. Universal availability through an aerial (rather than a cable or a dish) is only possible for four channels distributed by analogue signals. All other channels must depend upon multiple distribution mechanisms to reach anywhere near the 99.4% coverage enjoyed by those four. By the same token, however, all the additional channels have similar, if not quite total, coverage. Some are free-to-air, some are subscription or even pay-per-view funded: but all are equally available to the population at large, provided households are willing to pay whatever is required to receive them.

In that context, the BBC's services are no more universally available than any others, and reception of them is similarly conditional upon payment of the correct fee. That this fee is also payable by those households choosing additional pay services does not alter the principle involved. The refusal to allow the option of just choosing free-to-air advertising-funded services – which a subscription-funded BBC system would permit – further discriminates against the poorest homes.

The BBC's response to this is that allowing people to opt out of paying for and receiving BBC services would inhibit participation in collective viewing experiences; would deprive people of socially-valuable programming; and would undermine the BBC's finances.

Whatever value there might be in "collective viewing experiences" – a matter of some dubiety – it is hard to believe that it outweighs the right to opt out of a compulsory payment for an unwanted service. As for social deprivation, if governments really believe that BBC output has such positive social benefits, there can be no excuse for failing to supply such output through the general taxation system, as is done with some other "merit goods", such as education and health.

In terms of the BBC's finances, there is little doubt that a proportion of households – perhaps as high as 15% – would do without BBC services if payment for them were optional. However, there is also abundant evidence that BBC services are entrenched in people's viewing habits – taking up more than 10 hours a week of viewing, on average – and that a substantial part of the population would pay more for them than the current cost of the licence fee. Indeed, the sheer political inflexibility of a flat-rate charge that bears most heavily on the poorest has held back the BBC in two ways: it cannot expand the number of its services as it sees fit, nor can it offer flexible packages of services, let alone an a la carte choice. Nor can it seek – as it would in a rational broadcast market – to vary its prices in accordance with consumer demand.

To imagine – as some Cassandras do – that the BBC would collapse if people could choose to do without its television channels is remarkably pessimistic in the light of the constant reminders from the BBC of the tremendous value the licence fee represents. Indeed, the BBC regularly claims to be much better value than cable and satellite packages, contrasting a licence fee of just over £100 with a typical pay television bill of £300 a year. In truth, such a comparison between the purchasing power derived from a compulsory charge levied on 22 million households and that derived from a voluntary charge on 7 million households is profoundly misleading. But unless the BBC has been deliberately churning out false propaganda, it must surely be reasonable to conclude that the BBC would do well in the open market, and knows that it would.

However, even when embracing that likelihood, the BBC tends regretfully to pronounce that it would be wrong in principle to exclude – even by their own choice – that proportion of the population who might drop out if allowed to – however regressive and anti-social the mechanism for forcing them to stay in. But then, few organisations would willingly give up a guaranteed annual income of billions of pounds in order to submit themselves to the verdict of the consumer. Only technological advance may force the BBC's hand.

The licence fee was designed for the age of spectrum scarcity, as essentially a single charge for two channels. But as spectrum scarcity disappears in the digital age, and as the BBC's ambitions expand, the "one size fits all" approach is coming apart at the seams. The House of Commons Culture Committee – perhaps without realising it – put its finger on the key issue of the BBC in the digital age, in its comments on the most expensive new BBC channel, BBC Choice. "Original programming for BBC Choice poses a simple but fundamental question: why is such programming funded by the universal licence fee not available first on the BBC's universal channels?"

The debate over the digital licence fee has been exacerbated by the fact that it is an argument over different forms of unfairness which excludes the only fair solution – that all BBC television services should be individually priced and open to consumers to choose to pay for or not.

The paradox is that some BBC services are already operating in such a fashion. The BBC's joint venture with Flextech, UKTV, offers a number of public service channels, essentially made up of BBC repeats and assorted bought-in programmes. The most successful is UK Gold, originally set up in 1992 by an American cable company, Cox, along with the BBC and Thames Television. Interestingly, its launch straddled the Checkland/Birt handover, and the BBC's enthusiasm for this first venture into pay television visibly diminished as Birt took control. Indeed, the BBC declined to take up an offer of free equity at the same 20% level in a sister proposition, UK Living, shortly afterwards: a failure that has cost the BBC tens of millions of pounds.

When the oil exploration company, Flextech, moved into the cable and satellite business, taking over an increasing number of channels, it proposed to the BBC a broad joint venture, into which UK Gold (which it by then controlled) would be injected. Flextech would provide the cash to launch UK Horizons (a factual strand), UK Play (formerly UK Style, but now concentrating on comedy) and UK Arena (originally arts oriented, but now being re-launched as UK Drama).

All four channels are funded by a mixture of subscription and advertising, but are scheduled by the BBC, which also provides much of their content. Whether they constitute public service broadcasting is a moot point: but they demonstrate that Birt's early hesitations about possible compromising of the BBC's licence-funded purity were ill-judged.

More importantly, their very existence sharply inhibits the BBC's case for extra funding to launch new free-to-air channels. If channels with substantial public service content can be commercially funded, with consumers left to choose whether or not they wish to subscribe, what is so compelling about the BBC's other digital propositions that requires compulsory funding, either of all television viewers through the licence fee, or of all digital viewers through a digital licence fee, or – perhaps – all taxpayers through a direct grant, as with the World Service?

The free-to-air digital services the BBC has already launched provide little ammunition. The costly BBC Choice is a modest adjunct to BBC1 and BBC2, sometimes taking overspill coverage of sporting events licensed by the BBC. BBC Knowledge is an education service, but would-be providers of commercial educational services, like Granada, do not understand why the BBC should have any, let alone exclusive, access to public funds to pay for it. BBC Parliament – which essentially offers live coverage of proceedings at Westminster – is as close to pure public service as anything on offer: but, even at £4 million per annum, is surely more appropriately funded by the Treasury than by the licence fee.

BBC *News 24* is the longest established of these new services. It has attracted fierce criticism, not least from the Commons Culture Committee, which could not understand how a channel provided at the margin of an already hugely expensive news operation could cost nearly £54 million a year, when an editorially superior stand-alone service like Sky News costs less than £24 million a year. Greg Dyke has suggested that Sky understates the true cost of its news channel, and that *News 24*'s costs may have been over-stated: but anyone with knowledge of both organisations would strongly incline to the view that the opposite was the case.

BSkyB has shrewdly pointed out that News 24 fails all the tests the BBC itself laid down for providing new digital services: that they be widely accessible, that they have wide appeal, that they fill a market gap and that they be cost effective. If the BBC had simply decided to fill its empty late-night hours on BBC1 or BBC2 with rolling news, no-one – even Sky – could have objected. But launching a dedicated limited-circulation news channel, in detrimental competition with pre-existing commercial services one of which consistently out-rates it head-to-head, and at enormous marginal cost, has earned the BBC the most scathing criticism from the Commons Culture Committee: "we find it difficult to discern the justification for *News 24* in view of its huge cost and small audience – the BBC has failed totally to explain why the costs of *News 24* are so high in the context either of other news broadcasters or in the context of its total news budget".

The Committee's overall conclusions were deeply dismissive of the BBC's digital efforts and its role in the digital world. Other than praising BBC Online, which the Committee recommended be converted into a commercial service, there was scarcely a positive note in the Report it published in December 1999. The Committee's view was that the BBC "had singularly failed to make the case for a much expanded role in the digital era and consequently for additional external funding". The Report sharply rejected not just a digital licence fee, but any increase in the main licence fee outside the 5-year settlement that ran till 2002.

Additional scorn was poured on the BBC's inept attempt to switch from the bid for £700 million a year for new services it submitted to Davies, and the call for £730 million a year it made after the

Davies Report's publication, which clearly included substantial extra expenditure on existing services.

That the BBC had made such a woeful hash of its digital strategy – the "brilliant digital positioning", as Greg Dyke described his inheritance – must surely be blamed on John Birt. The assurances that all the BBC's digital plans could be funded from within the 5-year settlement; the promise that new digital services would cost the licence fee payer nothing extra; the repeated dismissal of a digital licence fee as a tax on innovation; the painfully unconvincing U-turn to endorse the digital licence fee; the poor quality and high cost of the free-to-air services launched; the grandiose and ill-thought-through proposals to Davies; the hubristic demands for money and status post-Davies – all these must be laid at his door.

Even the Internet strategy has been confusing: a commercial venture with ICL – beeb.com – has been outflanked by the BBC's own public service offering – BBC Online; a service funded primarily by the licence fee is used primarily by foreigners; a service claimed as an extension of public service broadcasting, free at the point of use, involves every customer in paying either a telephone company or an Internet service provider according to level of use; content is funded at a level which could not be justified by all its domestic commercial competitors combined. These competitors have accused the BBC of using licence fee funding to mark out new territory in its familiar imperial fashion, crowding out commercial efforts in the process. Why was the licence fee being used for this purpose?

And yet all the time an alternative funding model was at hand, which the BBC rejected with increasing vehemence. And all the time the logic of digital technology is rendering the BBC's limpet-like attachment to the licence fee increasingly redundant. Sometime in the second decade of the 21st century, all televisions will be equipped with digital equipment that allows transmission signals to be decoded. Analogue broadcasts will be ended. And it will be possible to disconnect any set electronically from access to channels for which payment had not been made.

Is it conceivable that in the digital century we will still have an army of detector vans, and millions of paper forms, when a smart card can do the job more efficiently? Will we still insist on a £250 million a year cost to the BBC of collection and evasion of the TV licence, when an electronic database controlling payments for BBC services would not only be fairer (in penalising evaders) and more cost-effective, but would also constitute a substantial business asset?

Once there is a mechanism for differentiating between consumer willingness to pay for different BBC services, we will find that they are correctly priced without our having to be told they are excellent value for money, and that the BBC can launch a whole series of targeted services without having to ask Flextech's – or the Secretary of State's – permission.

Basic BBC content will be cheaper for the poorest households; there will be no free-riders; the creative resources locked up inside the BBC will be released to their full potential; and without any need for privatisation, or profit-making – or even advertising between programmes – the BBC would flourish and be truly accountable.

The BBC has tried and failed to contain its ambitions for the digital age within its historic licence fee level of income. It has botched the case for a digital licence fee. It has been derided for its digital offerings and its huge claims for more cash. It has united virtually all its competitors in fierce opposition, in unprecedented fashion. It has been savaged mercilessly by a cross-party group of well-informed MPs.

The licence fee is with us for at least another decade. It has served the BBC well, for longer than many expected. But it is not a totem-pole to be worshipped. It works because the BBC works, not the other way round. And the BBC's ability to work at any politically realistic level of licence fee is increasingly in doubt.

In that context, the alternative method of subscription funding – which technology invites and compels, and which would confer on the BBC legitimacy, accountability and true independence – must surely soon find its way to the top of the agenda: in particular, that of the committee which, in the next two years, will be appointed as perhaps the last of the great post-war inquiries into broadcasting of which the first, by Lord Beveridge, reported half a century ago.

Lightning Source UK Ltd.
Milton Keynes UK
UKOW04f1223241115

263403UK00002B/11/P